Mastery of Non-Mastery
in the Age of Meltdown

MASTERY OF NON-MASTERY IN THE AGE OF MELTDOWN

Michael Taussig

The University of Chicago Press

Chicago and London

The University of Chicago Press, Chicago 60637
The University of Chicago Press, Ltd., London
© 2020 by The University of Chicago
Published 2020
Printed in the United States of America

29 28 27 26 25 24 23 22 21 20   1 2 3 4 5

ISBN-13: 978-0-226-68458-1 (cloth)
ISBN-13: 978-0-226-69867-0 (paper)
ISBN-13: 978-0-226-69870-0 (e-book)
DOI: https://doi.org/10.7208/chicago/9780226698700.001.0001

Library of Congress Cataloging-in-Publication Data

Names: Taussig, Michael T., author.
Title: Mastery of non-mastery in the age of meltdown / Michael Taussig.
Description: Chicago ; London : University of Chicago Press, 2020. | Includes bibliographical references and index.
Identifiers: LCCN 2019046588 | ISBN 9780226684581 (cloth) | ISBN 9780226698670 (paperback) | ISBN 9780226698700 (ebook)
Subjects: LCSH: Human ecology—Philosophy. | Nature and civilization. | Civilization, Modern—21st century. | Human ecology in art.
Classification: LCC GF21 .T38 2020 | DDC 304.201—dc23
LC record available at https://lccn.loc.gov/2019046588

♾ This paper meets the requirements of ANSI/NISO Z39.48-1992 (Permanence of Paper).

For a Green New Deal

The last night that she lived
It was a common night,
Except the dying; this to us
Made nature different

We noticed smallest things,—
Things overlooked before,
By this grand light upon our minds
Italicized, as 't were.

EMILY DICKINSON

CONTENTS

SMOKE AND MIRRORS

Speaking about the Green New Deal before a packed audience in the Bronx, late March 2019, Alexandria Ocasio-Cortes gave me pause when she said, almost as an aside, "It has an expiry date"

She meant the planet. Planet earth. "Our" planet, in some way

Such a smart way, such a mimetic way, of putting it, using the label on supermarket merchandise to label our destiny, bearing in mind that merchandise, meaning our economic system, is the root of the problem

We too can play that game, she is saying, that smoke and mirrors game

Like the dance. In her first days in Congress some Republicans posted a video of her dancing on a rooftop in Boston almost a decade earlier as a college student. Was it meant to wound, to make her look out of place, the Dancing Bartender?

Her response?

She mimicked the video. She made a video of herself dancing the same dance in front of her office in Congress

It went viral, copies chasing copies as in spirit worlds, changing their form and hence the rules of the game

We too can play that game, she is saying, that smoke and mirrors game, and if we play it right, we change the game

There is the mimetic element, the mirror. And there is smoke, mysterious and irritating, blending with reflections, setting up waves of metamorphic sublimity

The Trumpies talk of fake news, but who is faking who?

We too can play that game. Take the label from the supermarket and stick it on the world. The world looks different and smells different then, like an expired egg or a rotting chorizo. This we call mimetic excess

An expiration date on planet earth makes you reconsider a lot of stuff. "The last night that she lived," wrote Emily Dickinson,

We noticed smallest things,—

Things overlooked before

There is a new sense of connection and connectedness. Things come alive, resonating with the eerie fragility of newborn babes. You become aware of an amplification of the mimetic faculty as, with its changes in color and smell, a new sort of life surges through the dying egg no less than through the chorizo, as the yellow fat, tinged red, then brown, exudes from its intestinal wrapping

This I call "dark surrealism," our new real, which along with metamorphic sublimity is as present in the environment as in the White House and its clones throughout the world. Outside of myth and biblical terror, has there ever before been mimesis on this cosmic scale in which the turbulence of political power mirrors the turbulence of nature such that the sun itself ceases to give without receiving?

That is the subject of this book, as nature strikes back, re-enchanted, every day more strange, such that the amplification of the mimetic faculty therewith comes to include what I call the *mastery of non-mastery* and, with that, the possibility for mutuality in place of the colonization of nature and ourselves

Which, by the way, involves MNM writing that crosses over between writing and theater, which was how this all began long ago on the beach, and which, by the way, recruits stagecraft, trickery, and sub-terfuge of a high order summed up as the skilled revelation of skilled concealment, somewhere between science fiction, high theory, and the weather

Oh! and of course, knowing what not to know, as you shall soon find out

1 MIMETIC EXCESS

From the wheel to the atom bomb, from Mendel's peas to DNA, from shamans to Sergei Eisenstein's cream separator, we have excelled in mimicking nature so as to exploit it, just as we exploit each other and ourselves.

If I am correct in assuming that global meltdown amplifies mimetic and animistic impulses as never before, might mimetic excess provide us with a way out, providing a mutuality geared to the mastery of non-mastery, therewith giving the planet and ourselves a break?

Mimesis is a form of trickery as well as magic. Adorno put it rather beautifully—but then he had a beautiful subject—when he described Walter Benjamin's method, or was it a trick, as the need for everything to "metamorphose into a thing in order to break the catastrophic spell of things."[1]

My favorite example of mimesis is the human face, faced with another face as mask and window to the soul. How skilled we are at reading and responding facially, which here means acting, or should I say, feigning insensibly fast, subliminally mirroring reciprocities and anticipations.

But perhaps we should start with something simpler, like the mimesis between the wing of a bird and that of an airplane. Have you never wondered how a cross-section so cunning and simple can lift you off the ground? Now multiply this to infinity—lift off, I should say, start flying—for is not our world, both artificial and natural, a treasure trove of analogies and similarities? Are not these analogies alive with the reciprocating tension of the gift that binds them and endows them with empathetic force?

But if the bird's wing is a gift to civilization, what does the bird get in return?

That is the question.

Consider the mimetic faculty. In 1933 Walter Benjamin pointed to what he considered humans' loss of alertness to similarities in his essay "Doctrine of the Similar," followed months later by his essay "On the Mimetic Faculty." Little more than three pages each, these essays were ignored or smuggled *sotto voce* into major contributions to critical thinking, most notably Horkheimer and Adorno's riff on anti-Semitism in the Third Reich, their analysis of shamanism as an early attempt at the domination of nature, and Adorno's weighty aesthetic theory, in which Benjamin's idea of mimesis fuels a persistent train of thought.[2] In each of these instances, however, the mimetic faculty is treated like an embarrassing family member whose name is to be avoided but whom, at crucial times, proves indispensable.

"Nature creates similarities. One need only think of mimicry," begins Benjamin's essay on mimesis. "The highest capacity for producing similarities, however, is man's. His gift of seeing resemblances is nothing more than a rudiment of the powerful compulsion in former times to become and behave like something else."[3]

To become and behave like something else.

A bold statement. A statement those of us in an English-speaking tradition and coming out of anthropology would recognize as mimetic with what, in *The Golden Bough*, is called "sympathetic magic."[4] But for Benjamin the mimetic faculty goes further than what is generally meant by magic.

It is his thesis that over the long haul of Western history, from the ancient world to the present, the mimetic faculty, though still an active presence among children (and, we might add, in magical practices), has been largely eclipsed from conscious awareness. And not just eclipsed but actively repressed, as if it were dangerous, not only childish but barbaric, animal, inferior. Hence our term "aping" and Franz Kafka's astonishing story of Red Peter, an ape who was able to mimic humans and lecture to an academy in Berlin on what it was like to become human.

But given its essential role in human affairs, has the mimetic faculty really been eclipsed? Or has it, like a dammed river, found alternative routes? Benjamin suggests that "non-sensuous correspondences" provide mimetic links between things and activities not obviously mimetically related, and then he takes a further step, suggesting that language itself can be thought of in this way too.

For now, though, let me return to the bird's wing and that of the airplane to suggest a further and radical development in our time on account of changes affecting the mimetic faculty wrought by climate change. Now we are flying fast and high, mimetic beings in wonderlands of what until recently was pure make-believe. One minute it's winter, the next, summer. Tremors and drought shake the earth and its peoples, while the far-fetched notion that the real is really made up has become real. The bird's wing is different now. Transformation, mirroring, and boxes within boxes, as in a Harry Potter universe, best characterize our present dispensation. At the risk of being thought too fanciful, I call this situation "the metamorphic sublime."

Running through all of this is a colonial endowment of mimicry miming itself—what I call mimetic excess.

Let me explain.

In a darkened classroom around 1990, screening Jean Rouch's film *Les maîtres fous*, made in Ghana in 1955 just before independence. (Note the title: "the mad masters.") The film concerns migrants from the French colony of Niger enacting in trance the spirits of French officials, seen now in black bodies gesticulating wildly and disjointedly, eyes rolling, spume frothing from their mouths. They enact mini-dramas of transgression and of military discipline. Transgression and discipline conjoined! Fancy that! They eat dog and they carry (toy) rifles. They exult in the exercise of mastery over craven subjects crawling on the ground. The crucial point is that the bodies in trance are and manifestly are not the French officials. The bodies mimic, yet the result is not without parody, and parody (as Steve Feld once pointed out) is mimesis with one aspect accentuated, which is all you need for mimetic excess.[5] Yet even without accentuation, to be mimed is disconcertng. These men and women from Niger, part of the Hauka cult, thus bring out the wildness, the spirituality, and—most important—the sheer bluff their masters enact in the colonial theatricalization of mastery in general. Jean Genet's play *Les Negres* is based on this, gets its steam from this. To mime is to get the power of what is mimed *and* power over it. All that plus parody as well!

Then we screened Jerry Leach and Gary Kildea's film *Trobriand Cricket: An Ingenious Response to Colonialism*, filmed in 1972–1973. This shows Trobriand men enacting synchronized dance routines at dramatic moments during the game of cricket. One dance evokes sea birds darting over the waves, another, US bombers lifting off the tarmac in the Trobriand islands during World War II.

We are told that cricket was introduced by missionaries to displace war. (!) We could say that the game here is mimetic of war, at least in the opinion of the missionaries. The Trobrianders copied English cricket but added their own ideas, including magic, bowling with the same arm movements as hurling a spear, and allowing political agreements between rival chiefs to decide which team should win. Mimesis is always creative. (Deleuze and Guattari get it wrong when they insist it means direct copying.)

At what I take to be the crucial moments in each film, the magic of mimesis billows forth in jaw-dropping juxtapositions orchestrated by the film editor. In *Les maîtres fous*, an egg is cracked over the head of a small, painted wooden statue of the colonial governor placed among the entranced bodies, followed immediately by a shot of the British governor of Ghana stepping from his limousine during a state ceremony, displaying his hat of ostrich plumes, yellow with a white surround, like a cracked egg in a frying pan.[6]

In *Trobriand Cricket* we see dancers imitating sea birds, then footage of sea birds skimming the waves, then back to the dancers. We see dancers—crouched bodies arranged in lines, arms vibrating, magical plant leaf ornaments quivering—then footage of a World War II bomber (with the name, speaking of mimesis, birds, and airplanes, of "Squawking Hawk").

And we gasp.

I have thought a lot about that gasp, that in-drawing of breath when words fail, the body emptying out at the marvel of it all.

This reaction, I suggest, is more than an appreciation of filmmaking wit. It is a visceral reaction to a bodily history of the mimetic faculty, from the miming body in the colony to the mimetically capacious machinery in the metropole such as the movie camera. The gasp is not merely colonial history in a nutshell but a moment in which the mimetic faculty speaks for itself. The instrumental function of mimesis, used to colonize nature from the shaman's gestures, drugs, and chants to the atomic bomb is exceeded in this moment in a burst of sheer joy and wonder that I call the mastery of non-mastery.

Check it out for yourself, the filmic miming of miming itself!

2 THE EXPOSITION OF THE NON-DOGMATIC CANNOT BE DOGMATIC

Mastery of non-mastery is what Roland Barthes described as "an ethic, a guide to life lived through twinklings of tact in an anecdotal discourse recruited to outsmart mastery."[1]

This involves much by way of experiment and failure.

The first experiment, in 2008, was "Something Is Happening," a series of five-minute talks by four people organized by Jordan Crandall, who was teaching visual studies at a local university. The talks took place at locations two to three miles apart on the coast in southern California.[2]

We started on a beach. The speakers stood. The audience stood. The waves crashed. Language became something else.

Then we moved to a cliff-face, a forest, and lastly a town. In retrospect I see the talks as timed to the rotation of our planet, and hence tied to our bodies in relation to the sun.

Dusk evoked memories of how my mother, on the other side of the Pacific, used to say this was the saddest time of day, something I would hear and read often in my life and in literature: as the starting point in Manuel Puig's *Cae la noche tropical*, and as the endpoint in Virginia Woolf's *The Waves*.

But they wrote before.

Before Meltdown.

It was not only sadness, of course. Sunset was mixed with turning life over, just as the ground under our feet was turning. Things then are recalibrated with what filmmakers call the "magic hour." Animals put on a show. The owl of Minerva emerges, as Hegel points out in relation to historical knowledge, and sometimes your heart leaps as starlings in their multitudes wheel and somersault across the darkening sky, love poems maybe, ecstasy for sure, sheer joy it seems—what Bataille should have chosen as his symbol of *dépense*, meaning spending for the hell of it. It's even got a name that makes you shiver. Murmuration, it's called. In *Gravity's Rainbow*, the birds arrive ahead of the bombers and rockets. The radar operators call them angels.[3]

It was a largely unconscious knowledge I was tapping into, what I came to call *the bodily unconscious*, in which *the body came to mean my body, your body, and the body of the world*. We are solar-oriented creatures in so many ways without knowing it, but now with climate change, I believe, we are becoming more aware of our bodies and of how perturbing and interesting is our relation to the cosmos at large. It is not that the bodily unconscious becomes conscious or even partially conscious, for it could not function unless it remains unconscious. Its forays into consciousness have to be furtive and sporadic, so to speak, leaving tremors, which is what language and consciousness pick up on.

When I put it like this you have to wonder how we could ever have thought of language as separable from where and especially when it is happening We have language by the beach, language at the cliff-face, language in the town; language at dawn, midday, or dusk; language right here on this page.

There was another thought attached to this, the question of how innocent an act is it, really, to delve into the workings of the bodily unconsciousness. Might it not be better left alone, away from the attentions of Dupont USA, the US National Science Foundation, and Big Pharma? (Fat chance.)

The second experiment leading to this book was the "Sun Theater" performed with the fluctuant light of dusk in Helsinki, Berlin, and New York, where at the Whitney Museum, February 2013, the text was accompanied by Anni Rossi playing viola and piano, as well as by a masked dancer, Kyle Bukhari. Images were projected from outside through the floor-to-ceiling windows. Language became something else in this theater-piece pressing on ritual. And why ritual? There must have been a sense that the mastery of non-mastery has an affinity with snow falling through translucent images as a masked dancer winds through the audience, come what may.

The third experiment is the book before you, situated between science fiction, the weather, and high theory.

Enmeshed in the two previous happenings, it began as a hybrid object—part theater-script (left-hand page) and part commentary on the script (right-hand page)—but the script resisted the distinction between theater and commentary, make-believe and belief, wind and words. Such is the mastery of non-mastery, what Roland Barthes in his last lecture course, on "the neutral," described as an ethic, a guide to life lived through twinklings of tact in an anecdotal discourse recruited to outsmart mastery.[4]

But doesn't outsmarting mastery perpetuate mastery, if only in another form? This is what leads Barthes to say that *the neutral* refuses to dogmatize because the exposition of the non-dogmatic cannot itself be dogmatic.[5] This poses problems of exposition.

3 NIETZSCHE'S TUNING FORK, KAFKA'S SIRENS

Barthes's "twinklings of tact" resemble Nietzsche's tuning fork, which, touching the idols of culture, echoes their hollowness, thereby destroying them.[1]

In this case the tuning fork is predicated on the notion that mastery is a matter of guile, of foxes as well as of lions, what Hubert Murray, a colonial governor in Papua in the early twentieth century called "administration by bluff."[2] Mastery very much included looking the part; shaven, clean white duds, pith helmet, and all that. How else could a few hundred white men hold sway over hundreds of thousands of natives? But then there was that pesky anthropologist, Bronislaw Malinowski, whom the governor deemed a "German pederast" and who did not seem to care much for bluff. Not that sort, at least. He wore pajamas or oversize shorts that kept falling as he took photographs of the islanders, who called him not a German pederast but "the guy with loose shorts." Who knows what that did to administration by bluff? He had another nickname as well: Show-off, or Performer.[3]

Performer he certainly was (but aren't we all?), as when, toward the end of his fieldwork, he was photographed by his friend Billy the Pearler. Decked out in colonizing regalia—pith helmet and whiter-than-white trousers and a flowing, long-sleeve whiter-than-white shirt—he mimicked the White Man as Ethnographer in a series of *tableaux vivants* artfully staged to show off his interaction with the islanders, male and female.

In one tableau he sits on a log with a bunch of almost naked men fondling a long spatula inserted into a bulbous gourd on his lap containing lime for betel nut. They could be a bunch of high school boys playing with their dicks. In another he seems to be airborne, floating above the islanders. He could be a spook, a spirit. In still another he assiduously examines necklaces strewn over the naked bosom of a young woman. He seems very clinical, like a physical anthropologist or an evaluator from Christie's. Then there is the pose to end all poses with him tautly erect, hands aggressively on hips, gazing at a scantily clad sorcerer (so the caption says) who leans languidly against a palm tree, staring back at him. The erotic tension is unmistakable.

Labeled "Introduction to the Ethnographer" the tableaux seem not merely theatrical but a spoof of ethnography and its colonial entailment. We could call them "Sly-Dog Postcards from the Field, 1917."

But contrast that with other sly-dog tricks in the published monograph *Argonauts of the Western Pacific*, where Malinowski would have us believe he is blessedly alone on a desert island but for the natives as the ship that brought him sails over the horizon. In fact the island had its district officer, Bellamy, a medical student from Cambridge University, a long jetty, and a prison for those natives who resisted Bellamy's reforms. But Malinowski, as much as we, his readers, and anthropologists writing their own ethnographies, seem to need and enjoy such fictions. Similar tricks of the trade appear throughout *Argonauts of the Western Pacific*. He writes vividly, for example, of a Kula expedition, giving the impression of being together with Trobianders on board their canoes when in fact the Trobrianders forced him to follow behind because he affected the wind. That is another kind of performance, the one affecting the wind no less than the sleight of hand affecting the illusion off authorial presence.

You get the point? If you need a thief to catch a thief, then you'd do well to have a performer in pajamas or whiter-than-white kit to catch out a colonial governor. What Antonio Gramsci called "hegemony" can take only so much derisive humor. It was Murray's nightmare come true. His bluff was bluffed. But what more could you expect of a German pederast? Really!

In a similar vein, in 1937 Bertolt Brecht asked who rules in the Third Reich?

Fear rules, he replied, including the fear the masters feel that one fine day the multitude will disobey, yawn, and not even bother to look up.

The "brownshirts fear the man whose arm doesn't fly up and are terrified of the man who wishes them a good morning."

Driven by anxiety
They break into homes and search the lavatories
And it is anxiety
That makes them burn whole libraries. Thus
Fear rules not only those who are ruled, but
The rulers too.[4]

What Brecht's alienation effect achieves in this poem is to turn mastery against itself—and something more, something that has always made Brecht's theater and poetry resonate with strategic ambiguity, doubling guile back onto itself.

Given this trick, whereby tuning forks become hammers, it is small wonder that the poem ends by invoking a magical spell:

The house of Tar, the Assyrian, that mighty fortress
Which, according to legend, could not be taken by any army, but
When one single, distinct word was spoken inside it
Fell to dust.

The greatest trick of all here is poetic conceit. We suspend disbelief. We assimilate the fairytale of the one magic word as counterweight to the Third Reich's administration by bluff.

So strange this evocation of magic by our Marxist poet. It's really not his style, is it? But then has he not pulled off something grand? First, he turns the tables, asking us to reverse the gaze and dwell not on the fear felt by the citizenry but the fear felt by the masters. Such a simple step. But revelatory. Second, the resort to magic serves *as if to mimetically match the magic sustaining fascism*, which, like the fortress, is best tackled not from outside but from within.

This strategy fits well with what, seven years after Brecht's poem was written, the authors of *Dialectic of Enlightenment*, Horkheimer and Adorno (who detested Brecht), also in reference to the Third Reich, called "the organization of mimesis."[5] By this they referred in a very general sort of way to the hypnotic trance evoked in everyday slogans and rites as well as in the spectacular theatrics staged in Nuremburg (see Leni Reifenstahl's film *Triumph of the Will*), the point, as I see it, being the fascist welding of the mass into the body politic by means of mimetic connectivity and the sense of primitivism entailed in those rites, in that trance, and in mimesis itself. In which case we could say that mastery of non-mastery (MNM) is *the disorganization of the organization of mimesis*, with the masked dancer winding his way through the audience, come what may.

If along the lines of Brecht's poem we were to think of the Third Reich's fascism as a modernization of sympathetic magic, then the disorganization of its organization would be the work of counter-sorcery, perhaps along the lines Artaud set forth in "To Be Done with the Judgment of God," a censored 1947 radio broadcast in which language was transformed into screams and babble of a private secret-sacred language confronting what Artaud understood to be our bewitched cosmos.

But there is also that MNM silence left reverberating after Artaud's cries and rough-edged growl die away, leaving silence like John Cage's piano composition without a sound, confounding expectations while noise from the street or from inside your head fills the void and the abdominal muscles clench for the dancer's next twist.

"A man of twists and turns" says Homer about Odysseus, that master of guile who stuffs his oarsmen's ears with wax so they will not hear the Sirens' song, while he is bound to the mast. In *Dialectic of Enlightenment*, Horkheimer and Adorno interpret this tale as exemplary of the cunning required for domination and the costs it imposes both on slaves and on the master.[6]

The oarsmen cannot hear the beauty of the song. The master has his senses partitioned. He can hear but he cannot move in response to what he is hearing. He is still-bound. His senses are dislocated. No longer is he a unified sensory-motor apparatus. The music and its beauty become detached, autonomous entities.

But in true MNM style, Kafka comments that Homer got it wrong. What actually happened is that the Sirens, whose song can penetrate anything, stopped singing. They did this because silence was their greatest weapon, or perhaps because they were overcome by the bliss on Odysseus's face, so pleased was he with his guile in outsmarting them.

He had, says Kafka, actually stuffed his own ears with wax, not realizing that the song of the Sirens can penetrate anything. Hence he did not hear their silence, their greatest weapon. And before we can ask how do you, how can you, not hear silence?, Kafka adds that Odysseus "was so full of guile, was such a fox," that it is possible he was faking it, that his smiling at his own cleverness was itself an act held up to the Sirens and the gods as a sort of shield.

No wonder Kafka adds that "here human understanding is beyond its depths."[7]

Is that what MNM is, then, beyond the depths of human understanding, an unwinding of unwinding without end? Do twinklings of tact, alienation effects, and incessant contradiction involve at their core a mirroring, a mimesis, that turns vertiginously in on itself?

This MNM weave of doing and outdoing is highlighted by Nietzsche's unsettling question as to why we consider truth more important than deception, his point being that truth itself cannot be truthfully justified and that without the idea of truth there can be no deception, which he takes to be the lifeblood of existence.

For you only have to ask yourself carefully, "Why do you not want to deceive?" especially if it should seem—and it does seem!—as if life aimed at semblance, meaning error, deception, simulation, delusion, self-delusion, and when the great sweep of life has actually always shown itself to be on the side of the most unscrupulous swindlers.[8]

Thus affirms the scholar of antiquity, son and grandson of Lutheran pastors on both his mother's and his father's side. And if life aims at semblance and dissimulation, is that not magnified today with the surveillance state and Facebook, not to mention the machinations of Kremlin and White House? The very instrument with which you tap out messages day and night, your laptop computer, is in fact the wooden horse of Troy, only smaller and smarter.

What, then, of Walter Benjamin's mimetic faculty, also aimed at semblance, as all that is solid melts into wild mimeses along with wild weather, the sorts of mimeses Flaubert describes in *The Temptation of St. Anthony*? Through the eyes of the saint tempted by the devil (the Great Imitator), he describes a world given over to mimetic relays: plants no longer distinct from animals, insects identical to rose petals. Other plants are like stones and stones are like brains as stalactites become breasts.

This hermit's world has been the subject of famous paintings from the Middle Ages through the Renaissance to Max Ernst and Salvador Dali. But Flaubert's rendering, stimulated by the painting of Breughel the Younger that he saw in the Balbi collection in Genoa, is more than visual and more than tactile. *The saint wants to become what he sees.* "I feel like flying," he says, "swimming, yelping, bellowing, howling." *He wants to be inside everything*, to "drift away with odors, flow like water, vibrate like sound, gleam like light, and curl myself into every shape, to penetrate each atom, to get down to the depth of matter—to be matter."[9]

This fits the mimetic bill beautifully. Or horrendously. Take your pick. I refer to the twofold character of mimesis: first as visual imitation, as with a vision or a photograph, and second as bodily engagement, as with using your lover's hair or undergarment to magically draw nigh. Only here, with the saint, the phrase "bodily engagement" seems far too feeble.

The saint is mad, for sure, afflicted with the savage ecstasies of religion and being alone in his cave but for his visions. His mimeses are also mad, but does not our world today have as much religious and magical resonance as that of the AD third-century hermit in the Egyptian desert, for is not nature today enchanted or, rather, re-enchanted? Is this not obvious as our negative-sacred sun burns us to a crisp as nature turns more surreal each day with ominous green-yellow vistas and bluer-than-blue skies while the snow falls one day, rising the next as mist, stripping us naked as pixies as the cosmos draws close?

The closest rendering of this new world of ours is the *Temptation of St. Anthony* triptych painted by Hieronymus Bosch between 1520 and 1530. While commentaries abound, I would point to the mix of fusion *and* rupture of hybrid forms made of animals, fish, birds, humans, and plants, enveloping and dismembering each other often in extraordinarily sexualized maneuvers. Is this then the metamorphic sublime?

Breughel the Younger's rendition of the saint is dark and moody. The emphasis is on the strange light rather than on the diminutive creatures that, like goblins or pet animals, surround the saint. The light is that of magic hour torn apart, as it were, by cosmic trauma. The saint is but a tiny figure crouched over a large book that absorbs all his attention. A large wooden dwelling forms much of the background. It is not only on the verge of collapsing but is merging with the nature around it, with a massive boulder and a twisted, fossil-like tree. It is easy today to read this as the collapse of the human-made world, flecked by a mordant sky.

Our desert today is not the Egyptian one, famously home to European magics. Ours is fulsome in the death-space of planetary demise, to which the bodily unconscious reacts furiously, or should I say creatively, attempting to stabilize an unstable world, leaving traces and tremors in consciousness as in this book you hold in your hands of traces and tremors, if book it be.

If book it be, as all manner of connections, mimeses, and metamorphoses sublime are aroused. Not just brains as stones, not this time around, but mimetic excess, meaning mimesis doubling back on itself, guile heaped on guile as in Kafka's rewrite of the Sirens.

Such is the overload of mimetic delirium and metamorphic sublimity that the organization of mimesis as the basis of the domination gives way to its disorganization through the mimicry of mimicry.

This then is MNM, poised on the edge of understanding, an unwinding of Hegel's master-slave parable by means of a left-handed reading of that parable such that the outcome is never secured and the dialectic never closes. It is set instead into a restless resistance staring death in the face, in which situation, as Hegel says in his famous preface to *The Phenomenology of Spirit*, miracles occur, and if not miracles, then magic—or even licentiousness as in Joseph Losey's 1964 film *The Servant*, based on the script by Harold Pinter.

Here the servant triumphs over the master and does so in a decidedly MNM way. It is a triumph in which master and servant transform their relationship into one of incongruous equals in a never-ending homosexual, or at least homoerotic, debauchery, mocking each other and playing games like children or drunks at each other's expense. It is as if all the demons of servitude, its guile, deceit, suffering, humiliation, and self-immolation, have surfaced and exploded in hallucinatory, play.

If anything, the servant has the edge in these games, but both (ex) master and (ex) servant seem to fall head over heels in love with each other and with the theater they jointly create of their new-found utopia.

Actually, they seem most in love with the game, with its seesawing changes of scene and power positions, rather than with any outcome. It is funny and erotic, everything Hegel is not. It is also scary. The theater they construct and keep on constructing seems as if it will wind on forever, just as the mastery of non-mastery keeps unwinding the many layers of paradox by which it is constituted and by which it is energized, hence the sex and play.

I keep wondering what would happen, however, if a visitor arrived? Would the servant resume the servant position as camouflage, like the dissimulating slaves in Melville's story of slavery and mimesis called "Benito Cereno," in which the cargo of African slaves who have taken command of the ship act as if they are slaves when another ship approaches? As I recall, Melville brings his talent to bear on the uncanny atmosphere felt by a white visitor to the ship who senses something amiss but cannot figure out what it is. This is the theater of dissimulation played for high stakes indeed.

What both "Benito Cereno" and *The Servant* bring out is not merely the theatrical element of power, which Brecht's poem "Who Rules in the Third Reich?" alerts us to so well, but the skilled revelation of skilled concealment that seems as inseparable from mastery as is its confrontation.

4 TWILIGHT OF THE IDOLS

"Like you I must *go down*," Nietzsche has Zarathustra say to the sun. "I must descend into the depths, as you do in the evening when you go behind the sea and still bring light to the underworld too, superabundant star!"[1] The word he uses for going under is *untergang*, which means

- the setting of the sun,
- drowning,
- and above all . . . perishing.

Perishing? Could it be that bad? Could our lives even today be so connected to the sun that we sense—every day, that is—intimations of death? Are we that archaic? Are we tied to a daily rhythm of death and resurrection without knowing it other than through some vague sense of dread as the day draws to a close and shadows lengthen?

As for drowning, is that because of the elemental connection between sunset and water?

We see this in the freak combination of sun and rain calling forth rainbows and a procession of foxes with broad flat hats like suns in Akira Kurosawa's film *Dreams*.

If you see them, says the little boy's mother, you will die. But it doesn't seem real, does it?, with that slanting light and tinkling sound as the rain bends with the sun, the little boy so fearless, and the end—well there is no end, not like the word "sink," which is what we use in connection with the sun and water, like when we say, "the sun sank in the west," whether there be water or not.

The most frequently evoked of all sinkings is the sun setting into an iridescent sea in a blaze of flame. That's how it is with Nietzsche and why Luce Irigaray called her book *Marine Lover*, homage to this brooding man of huge moustache and liquid prose setting your hair on end. What was the title of that last book? *Twilight of the Idols*?

Twilight?

Why twilight? (And before that he wrote *Dawn*.)

Is it because twilight marks the end of the day, the end of the day of the idols, for instance? Or is it because the light at that time of day ("magic hour") is curly, suggesting that the idols will never disappear, that life, politics, and philosophy depose idols (meaning metaphysical schemes) only to see new ones arise, such that the task of the philosopher is a never-ending magic-hourness aware of its half-lit qualities and stalking shadows?

Use a tuning fork as a hammer, Nietzsche says—this same Nietzsche who wanted to go to Mexico to experience fierce electrical storms to cure his fierce migraines. All philosophy, he suggested, is ultimately an interpretation of the body, then hastened to correct himself: a misunderstanding of the body is what he meant.

I think of the light of twilight and dawn as this same misunderstood body. It is certainly more than our everyday consciousness of light. If anything, it is an unconscious of light, if such be possible or plausible; more like nomadic movement through that "breath of empty space" that Nietzsche invokes with his "death of God." After all, this God is also the dying sun that has us "straying as through an infinite nothing" in a physics of sheer becoming in which being and non-being are transformed into the being of transforming forms.

Though the metaphors be compelling you might one day ask yourself, Does the sun really *set*? Is not the grandeur of twilight and dawn based on a marvelous illusion? For it is not that the sun descends but that our planet rotates west to east. It is strange that this rotational movement results in the illusion of a vertically setting sun. No wonder the light is strange at that time, subject as it is to these unseen trajectories. Soles glued to the earth we are nonetheless flying as if grabbed by the hair and hauled into the oblivion of the night as the sun appears to sink below the horizon, all at play in the magnificent illusion that orients our everyday self.

The shadows of magic hour highlighting and dissolving reality are the product of this illusion, this crisscrossing of cosmic cycles. No wonder people stare at the setting sun in mesmerized wonder.

What Nietzsche should have said, what would have better suited his drift, is that all philosophy is a misunderstanding not of the body but of the body in relation to the sun. I still see him under his umbrella, rain or shine, walking his walk everyday, thinking like lightning in Mexico.

But now the future is dark, and although it is ten o'clock in the morning, the sun, if there is a sun, has gone. The storm is about to break. Lisa stops to tell me the news at the first drops of rain. Like a magician she pulls a raincoat from her bag; it unravels and takes shape, dark hood and all.

The light is strange now, that of dawn or twilight, when space and time dissolve. But it's not dawn. It's not twilight. It is ten o'clock in the morning but the message seems clear—that with planetary destruction magic hour fitfully expands in stops and starts through the brain stem of being, or what's left of the brain stem of being, now transmuted into a light show rippling with urgent, low-flying birds.

And now mid-morning, with Lisa unraveling her raincoat, Hurricane Irene flattens the Bahamas and lumbers toward the city of New York at fourteen miles per hour but blowing at over one hundred. "Don't panic!" says the mayor. Old folk in low-lying areas by the sea are being evacuated. They are being evacuated from Coney Island, where the poor live alongside Ferris wheels and ghost trains. They are being evacuated from Battery Park, where people with money live not far from where the Twin Towers once stood. ("And we thought we were safe.") It is said the sea will rise with an eight- to ten-foot surge. Some places fifteen.

Upstate the baker in his long white smock tells me, "Long Island is being evacuated," as he hands me my change. He speaks with authority, as if bakers know storms like they know yeast. His bread is excellent. His face, pasty white. His eyes, glowing coals. His height, towering. Something's afoot, that's for sure. The normal looks anything but.

A girl with her hair covered by a bandana is painting the front of the old hotel with the American flag hanging on it. Still thirty-six hours to go.

On TV the dread-in-joy scenarios we have learned through the course of life come and go in spurts of the non-ordinary preparing us for the end, lifting the ocean that surfers in North Carolina dare to ride, laughing all the way.

There is a message on a giant sheet of plywood: *Good Night Irene*. But the plywood sheet nailed across the window says more than what's scrawled across it.

Red and orange generators are being unloaded for sale in mega-stores. It's war. It's play. Don't panic! Pickup trucks are loading jerry cans of gas and drinking water. And shot from real low—the ominous perspective—oracular red and orange taillights blink at us from SUVs stuck in traffic jams, mile after mile of evacuees fleeing the horror they have themselves intensified through years of un-seemly emissions. Makeshift human beings unable to walk, having given it up years ago. Walk? What's that? And what are they thinking to themselves locked in their barely moving vehicles?

Evacuation is the word you hear from all quarters, like that woman speaking loud into her cell phone in the queue at one of those big-box stores brought to New York City by the zero-tolerance mayor—was that his name? Duane Reade?—ghostly places taken over by zombie clerks and zombie customers, where you would be lucky to hear a human voice . . .

But now!

Evacuation! Evacuation!

she keeps on saying. A new word, a new tongue, another language we are only beginning to learn.

From his vacation on Martha's Vineyard the president says, "All in-dications point to this being a historic hurricane."

As the bus tears out of the city through the tunnel under the Hud-son, the afternoon of the earthquake in August five days before Hur-ricane Irene came our way, the mood is jubilant. At least we got out, they are saying, these people who normally pile bags on the seat so that no one will sit by them now emphasizing the "we." At least *we* got out. Upstate the siren created for the Cold War out of fear of the Ivans bleats continuously as the volunteer firemen—backbone

of the Republican Party and the Conservative Republican Party—
sharpen their tools.

Each day people are more skittish; another pulse is beating, yet
within a couple of months nobody remembers.

5 CATASTROPHE: THE SOLAR INVERSION OF SATANIC DENIAL

Given that the fantastic power of catastrophe is the new normal, it is strange so little attention is paid to the startling quality of new experience that is life today and what that means for representation itself. We seem stuck in a nightmare we cannot express, "at the apex of a thought," as Bataille put it, "whose *end* jumps the rails on which it is travelling."[1] Worse still is how we manage "to substitute empty thinking for those moments when it seemed to us, however, that the very heavens were opening."[2]

Prisoners of codes evolved in pre-meltdown time, we are locked into the normal, not its exception. But then how do you invent a new cultural form geared towards the exception as the rule? How do you handle the apex of a thought that jumps the rails given that you too are part of such a jump? Is the problem, therefore, not the need for a new culture—a "culture of catastrophe"—but the need for something like the mastery of non-mastery that doubles back on itself, so to speak, a twisting logic that meets at least halfway the exception as the rule?

Here I am mindful of the fact that Bataille expended an all-consuming effort to confront the unrepresentability of catastrophe, claiming it was impossibile to give it voice. In his 1963 homage to Bataille, Michel Foucault takes up the challenge with poetic prose like the following, writing of transgression as "the solar inversion of satanic denial" that is

like a flash of lightning in the night which, from the beginning of time, gives a dense and black intensity to the night it denies, which lights up the night from the inside, from top to bottom, and yet owes to the dark the stark clarity of its manifestation, its harrowing and poised singularity; the flash loses itself in this space it marks with its sovereignty and becomes silent now that it has given a name to obscurity.[3]

Well! That certainly would help explain our muteness faced with catastrophe as transgression! Contradiction is heaped on contradiction with an almost loving gesture, not to resolve anything—no! not at all—but so as to allow further irresolution to ripple. More than logic, in the usual sense of the word, is the poetry. More than idea is sensuous experience and its utterly transitory character canceling itself out no sooner than it occurs. Such is the mastery of non-mastery—not so much transgression as its mimetic confrontation, as when Foucault writes of transgression as the liberation of our language as it refers "to itself and is folded back on a questioning of its limits as if it were nothing more than a small night lamp that flashes with a strange light, signaling the void from which it arises and to which it addresses everything it illuminates and touches."[4]

Let us pause a moment to register the essential components here involved. First the continuous references to the play of light and dark and their mutuality—as with the cinematographic enthusiasm for the "magic hour" of twilight and dawn. After all, was not the sun the central figure in Bataille's writings?

Second, the "negation of negation" that occurs as transgression is deemed as liberating language, especially nondiscursive language. In other words, the nightmare of meltdown and its throttling of speech and representation turns out to be a force that opens up new language and new forms of response, evocation, and being.

Foucault's stalking horse here was sexuality as transgression, as if transgression itself had become transgressed. Essential here was the argument that the very notion of the limit, the very notion of transgressing the limit, was suspect, more a plaything of "dialectics" that only mystified the irregularities of language and the disappearance of the speaking subject.

Now, almost sixty years after that essay, has not meltdown taken the place of sex, not to mention "the death of God," or at the least reconfigured them?

No one seems to get this better than President Trump, as when in April 2019 he denounced US congresswoman Ilhan Omar as "a sick monster." His hate speech, amplified and protected by his bully pulpit, is mimetic beyond belief. He is what he denounces. His "sympathetic magic" rebounds onto himself. "Extremely unpatriotic," he adds. "Extremely disrespectful of our country. This from a man who claimed five exemptions to avoid being drafted into the Vietnam war and could not stop denouncing John McCain as a loser even after McCain's death. The killing of fifty Muslims by an Australian white supremacist in Christchurch, New Zealand, a month before on March 15, 2019, remains a vivid memory. But when questioned, the president is unperturbed that his statements appear to have led to death threats against Omar and seem to have played a role in the massacre in El Paso August 3 of that same year.

He seems so spontaneous. He rearranges reality, splicing amputated quotes to amputated quotes to be joined to flashes of videos spliced to other flashes of videos. Montage—a revolutionary art style when, long ago in Weimar Germany, the communist John Heartfield used scissors and paste to rearrange script and images culled from the capitalist press—has not only long been coopted by advertising but now, in our own "Weimar" of 2019, has become ever more powerful, ever more shameless, ever more "shamanic," reminding me of Carl Schmitt's notion that the exception, the breaking of the rule, is far more relevant and interesting than the rule itself. "Sovereign is he who decides on the exception," reads the first sentence of his book *Political Theology*.

It is a dangerous moment. You feel the world tremble. And it has been like this for a while. At least since 9/11. There is no more ordinary. The whole world is living not just another era but another culture. We cannot process what is happening, and that applies to both left and right on the political spectrum. As the end approached, the dinosaurs must have had the same problem of representational inertia.

How do you, how can you, represent the unbelievable, the deliberately unbelievable, the deliberately transgressive, like the recorded boast of pussy-grabbing that I take to be a defining act of this presidency. With that we are cast onto seas of great nothingness, as when Nietzsche wrote of the death of god: "Who gave us the sponge to wipe away the entire horizon? What were we doing when we unchained this earth from its sun? Whither is it moving now? Whither are we moving? Away from all suns?"[5]

Interpretations of this famous text are legion and change according to circumstance. Today I read it as encapsulating a new political style congruent with a new natural environment. "Are we not plunging continually?" it goes on. "Backward, sideward, forward, in all directions? Is there still any up or down?"

Nietzsche continues: "Are we not straying, as through an infinite nothing? Do we not feel the breath of empty space?"

And what is this space? Is it not the mastery of non-mastery or an approximation thereof?

In the first sections of *Journey to the End of the Night*, Céline writes with this insight, as does Pynchon in *Gravity's Rainbow*. Both engaged horror with absurdity. It was not that they used absurdity against horror. The absurd was in the horror. What they did was refashion the horror and thus deflect catastrophe by turning it against itself. Trump, after all, is a parody of himself. Brecht comes up with the same therapeutic in "The Anxieties of the Regime," in which as a final stroke he invokes a fairytale, and Beckett is in there too as we wait for Godot and the sunset.

But most of all here I like Simone Weil and her short tract *The Iliad; or, The Poem of Force*, where she writes, "Only the person who has measured the dominion of force, and knows how not to respect it, is capable of love with justice."

I like it because I think knowing how not to respect force is extremely difficult.

I like it because taking the measure of force suggests not only an intimacy with that which is to be confounded, but a delicate mirroring of it that converts it into something quite else.

And I like it because, along with the notion that justice without love falls short of justice, there is recognition of the sacred and magical qualities of the catastrophe, what Bataille thinks of as sacred horror and Julia Kristeva, in *Powers of Horror*, refers to as abjection, one characteristic of which is a breakdown of the barriers between self and other, as in an imploded mimesis.

Above all, when Bataille writes that sacrifice consecrates that which it destroys, I take this to be applicable to the consecrating power of destruction. Perhaps this is the point, intellectual and emotional, that I am striving to express. That catastrophe, as with meltdown, environmental as well as political, is permeated with sacred and mythical force.

Bataille makes much of the task of finding a language that can measure up to the "too muchness" of extreme experience. And yet his entire approach, it seems to me, rests on the notion that we fail, unable ever to be freed from Nietzsche's questions regarding the death of god. "Are we not straying, as through an infinite nothing? Do we not feel the breath of empty space?"

But then there is surrealism—at least Bataille's variation thereof—and there is his lead poet and painter writing songs of innocence, William Blake, who had a remarkable eye for the re-enchantment of nature, of which he never lost sight. In fact the epigraph to Bataille's *The Accursed Share* is a quote from Blake: "Exuberance Is Beauty."

Is it by chance that most of the writings in Bataille's surrealist period had to do with the body in relation to the cosmos, especially the sun? Is it by chance that alongside those short writings, or should I say prose poems and provocations, was the long-to-the-point-of-tedious essay on the psychological structure of fascism? In the humdrum language of today we would describe this essay as having an environmental focus joined to a political economic focus, noting that in Bataille's case the former involved a surreal take on the body-and-cosmos, the latter on a dogged pursuit of what would he later would call "general economy," with its emphasis on "unproductive expenditure."

We might also note that these early writings occurred within art, as in the famous journal *Documents*, which Bataille edited. This is an important observation, as art here indicates a call for a "beyond" of philosophy and social science where body-and-cosmos meets fascism—our present dispensation.

This is probably why I realized, suddenly, while writing this tract concerning MNM, that I have actually been tracing the submerged presence of the re-enchantment of nature, which in turn entails the metamorphic sublime and a dark surrealism. These concepts themselves depend on a specialized or, if you prefer, eccentric vocabulary made up of what I call "shamanic tropes," such as "the skilled revelation of skilled concealment," "knowing what not to know," "the bodily unconscious," "magic hour," and of course the lead dancer itself, "mastery of non-mastery."

As regards the *metamorphic sublime*, I have in mind the example of Trumpism as a shorthand for the sleight-of-hand theatricality of today's politics, just as I have in mind our environment as in a state of metamorphic frenzy. What is painfully obvious today is how stupendously well Trumpism mimics the shudder of environmental meltdown. They are variants of each other, mimetic to a fault, starting with the administrative chaos, orange hair, and pear-shaped corpus wading across the South Lawn while the cameras roll and a marine helicopter, engine roaring, makes the journalists' questions inaudible. "Can't hear! Can't hear!" he shouts, pointing to the chopper that like a magic carpet shall loft him heavenward. The chopper, you might recall, was the preeminent symbol of the Vietnam war, and nothing, says Michael Herr in his account of that war, was as magical as the helicopter.[6] I myself used to hear them, generously gifted by Bill Clinton, woop woop across the mountainsides as the shaman was singing along the Mocoa River, curing adults afflicted with sorcery or kids with the spirits of the dead. A strange sound like wings flapping, not that different, perhaps, from the spirits of the dead.

To call Trump's behavior "theatrical" is beyond obvious. To call it "inspired" is to my mind no less true and is what makes me want to conflate certain aspects of my fieldwork in Colombia since 1969 with the Trump White House and with the sort of world the latter grew out of, especially Murdoch's Fox News and the hallucinatory reality it creates (equal to that of the shamans' plants).

My overarching idea is "shamanic" in the sense of the actual hallucinogen-based shamanism I experienced living with Santiago Mutumbajoy in visits from 1972 to the late 1990s in the foothills of the Andes in the Putumayo River basin of Colombia. What was hallucinatory in ritual involved multiple realities cascading into each other's othernesses, along with fluctuating paranoia amid uncertainty and bodily fragmentation carried aloft by the shaman's song in stops and starts the night long. There could be a lot of laughter, a lot of crying, and lot of trauma, yet in that very trauma, as with the mastery of non-mastery, lay the seeds of cure—which is to say, cure from sorcery, which is, to say the least, desperately needed in the USA today.

When I first went to the Putumayo in 1971, I was amazed at the amount of sorcery that existed there. Like so much in anthropology, a statement like this is actually an implicit comparison with Western middle-class life, but now, in 2020, I need to revise my opinion. If we think of sorcery as a simplified term for a keen sense as to invisible maleficence—as with "fake news" or, more to the point, with the attribution of "fake news—then we can discern how a figure like Trump, buoyed up by the magic of the presidency ("In God We Trust"), finds his mojo.

As for "multiple realities," this was something I coined in response to the many different accounts offered by locals in the agribusiness fields of the Cauca Valley, where I have visited every year since 1969. These were accounts concerning the corpses of people who had made a misstep in drug deals, found weekly by the roads leading into town. Sometimes, so it was said, their lips would be sewn together and the marks of torture evident. Each story led to many more, and the narrators rarely agreed with one another. Hanging over all of these stories was an atmosphere as impenetrable as it was invisible, as palpable as it was insubstantial (reread Foucault's gloss on Bataille's philosophy of transgression).

It was pretty much the same with the widely differing accounts told me by peasants and landless workers about the colonial origins of miracle-working saints in the Cauca Valley. How might these be connected, these saints and murder, miracles of the colonial church and mysteries of malignity?

This multiplicity of stories destabilized me and the moorings that, up to that time, I thought I required for sociological reckoning. Wasn't it our job to create order out of disorder? Reason itself dictated such. But then what to do with the empirical reality of multiple realities, of what is now in the USA is called a "post-truth" era? Later it seemed to me that a more cinematic and a less sociological mode of reckoning was required of me, a mode attuned to what is called montage, in which different realities and different images are juxtaposed one to the other. This goes beyond vision to include the body of the perceiver as much as the body of the perceived, as with Cubism, in which Renaissance perspective focusing the object into the eye of the beholder is displaced by multiple points of view and colliding surfaces.[7]

Thus, it was that the "shamanic" world, hitched to those multiple realities, was much on my mind, and especially so from the late 1980s onward as paramilitaries sprang into action, paid for if not directly organized by rich people who took seriously Mao's dictum about guerrilla armies being like fish living in the sea that is the peasantry. The solution? Massacres, of entire villages if need be. And the priest as well, preferably with power-saw amputations, limb by limb while he is still alive. The really sickening thing, however, was that not only the rich supported this but, as the Colombian equivalents of Fox News ramped up their US-friendly message about narcoterrorism, the petty bourgeoisie of small towns were all too eager to go along with the paramilitaries' depredations, including the assassination of young people in gangs.[8]

The "shamanic" element in all of this lay in the clouds of uncertainty and rumor, which brings me in turn to the seemingly all-too-easy target of Trump, bearing in mind that this all-too-easiness is part of what makes the toxic brew toxic. In an era constantly belly-aching about the need for transparency, is not our Shaman-in-Chief the epitome, such that yes! you really can see straight through him.

Of course, Trump is only part of a whole, but is he not a necessary part of what I have shamanically in mind regarding dodge and feint and a larger-than-large theatrical presence verging on the grotesque that is magical if not sacred, this dissembling creature denigrated by his first secretary of state as a fucking moron and by others of exalted rank as an idiot? They were right, of course, but they were wrong too. Having the whole of the Republican Party and the Supreme Court and the attorney general in your hands makes you very smart. The deposed head of the FBI, an organization as sinister as you can get, put it well, as only a victim mimetically in synch with his antagonist could: "Speaking rapid-fire with no spot for others to jump into the conversation," noted James Comey, "Mr. Trump makes everyone a co-conspirator to his preferred set of facts, or delusions. I have felt it—this president building with his words a web of alternative reality and busily wrapping it around all of us in the room. . . . And then you are lost. He has eaten your soul."[9]

This is FBI "shaman-speak" at its best.

The great faker is never more at home than when calling others fakes, lambasting "the failing *New York Times*," and never more at home than when labeling a Muslim congresswoman "a sick monster." This strikes me as what I often imagine sorcery to be like, what Comey with precision calls eating your soul, weaving a web of confusions, as when a shaman is said to be killing someone through magic. (I say "imagine" because you never really know if and when a sorcerer is at work.) Generally the sorcerer will be another shaman, and generally the ball bounces back and forth in billowing uncertainty such as we see on our screens day and night regarding the Trump White House—a crossword puzzle of contradiction described as chaotic, dysfunctional, and so forth. This emphasis in the media on dysfunctionality really misses the point. Comedians do not.

But unlike shamans, who exist in nonhierarchical societies, there can only be one Shaman-in-Chief in the USA.

What I sense here—and I could go further—is a hallucinatory world of things become other things—namely, the metamorphic sublime. With Amazonian shamans the paradigmatic case would be the shaman becoming a jaguar or a boa, but that's just the tip of the iceberg in a world given over to flux of being.

The role of the theatrical image is crucial. "Can't hear! Can't hear!" he bellows as the chopper drowns out the journalists. With the shamanism I know, the power of the image is the result of hallucinogens and song as well as of the colonial endowment of power projected onto the Indian of the forest mimetically retroacted back onto those seeking cure. In the case of our media, it is the result of manipulations so hallucinatory that they cannot even be recognized as hallucinatory but are deemed normal.

Pervading this sorcery world is the irradiative phlegm of the negative sublime, casting our world into ever darker surreality. In Paris in 1939 the members of the Collège de Sociologie around Bataille brought together surrealism and anthropology with generous infusions of Marx, Nietzsche, and Freud. Focused into their research project into fascism, this bore the name *Sacred Sociology*. Crucial here was the idea of the sacred as like the nervously nervous nervous system in its neurotic pulsing from attraction to repulsion and back again, enmeshed in its dedication to the secret that today we figure as the Mueller Report, collusion with Russia, phone calls to the Ukraine, peeing on the Obama bed in a Moscow hotel, Stormy Daniels, the Deep State, Trump's IRS returns, his SAT scores, his weird military service–deferring feet, the origins of his wealth, not to mention the kids' security clearances, what went on one-on-one with Putin, and so forth. As with any public secret, the power generated by all of this lies not with the exposure of the secret so much as its prolonged and forever incomplete semi-exposure, which in itself speaks of considerable artistry, all the more impressive for being semi-conscious, at best.

A common question is how come so many millions of people in the USA support Trump and why Trumpism is ascendant in much of the world? There are many responses to this question, such as racism and neoliberalism, but for me it is the irradiative phlegm of the negative sublime that constantly springs to mind.

All of which is to say that the frequently quoted idea of the *disenchantment of nature* has been overturned by our newly charged era of *re-enchantment*.

Here we should bear in mind that disenchantment and its connections with liberal secularism and the instrumental rationality of the modern state apparatus was never a fait accompli and never could be. Disenchantment existed and continues to exist but did and does so alongside continuous re-enchantment. It's not that cults and the church exist alongside the secular but that the latter itself is necessarily infused with its own magic, as argued in detail in Horkheimer and Adorno's *Dialectic of Enlightenment*. Enchantment was at the core of the new reality in industrializing Europe, but no longer was it deemed spiritual or magical. Nevertheless it was vital to the economy, as with Marx's commodity fetishism, the "religion" of work and productivity, the belief in progress, and, since World War II, the spirituality of consumerism, a fine example of which today is to walk to your boarding gate in any airport or through the El Paso Walmart where, in August 2019, a massacre occurred. As for the ramped-up racism sweeping the world, can you imagine anything more enchanted than white supremacism? It is crazy to think that disenchantment is a major player in today's world. In terms of re-enchantment, how different are the dreams of an ISIS caliphate and Trump's MAGA, fueled by tirades about the infidel—in the latter case, Mexican rapists and murderers, and of course their children?

For those of us who oppose this tooth and nail it seems that language and imagery fail us when we most need them, and do so spectacularly in a liberal, secular environment, especially an academic one. This is what makes Walter Benjamin's attitude, both magical and secular, so timely and fascinating.

Of course, the terms "magical" and "secular" here are secondary to style and voice, which, for Adorno, lay in what he saw as Benjamin's mimetic prose and the need to metamorphose into a thing in order to break the catastrophic spell of things.

Something else comes into play with re-enchantment, something that makes us perk up, listen more, see more, be aware like never before as to what is happening. The world acquires strangeness and we start exploring like when we were kids.

Like in the 1940s when we would crouch in front of the radio in Sydney after school each day and listen to "Tom the Naturalist." We found his stories fascinating. Spellbound, we were. Later, when I was a lot older, at university, there he was in the flesh, spending what seemed like hours before his lectures drawing elaborate zoo-logical diagrams in colored chalk on the blackboard that stretched all along one wall, drawings that would, at the end of the class, be erased. Bang! Gone! As if Michelangelo had erased and repainted the ceiling of the Sistine Chapel for each day's congregants. This was performance art *avant la lettre*.

We barely noticed, but today Tom the Naturalist's drawing and its matter-of-fact erasure would draw a lot of attention. Now I think about it, the same thing happened in the steeply tiered anatomy lec-ture theater; on a massive blackboard were elaborate colored chalk drawings of muscles and joints drawn that morning, nerves and layers of fascia accompanied by rat-a-tat lectures that took the art of descriptive prose to unimaginable heights. We took it for granted. And then came PowerPoint. The name says it all. A terrifying de-struction of the imagination.

Looking back decades later I might have thought "Pure Bataille," with all that excess, all that wasting through erasure. Maybe I would have paused and thought too about the billowing mimetic excess expressed by the radiant animation, a frog or a dogfish, its digestive system minutely elaborated in colored chalk, come alive before our eyes, swimming there on the blackboard.

My lifetime has witnessed the replacement of the magic nature held for the child by indifference. But now, sixty years later, Tom the Naturalist has once more become a focus of bated-breath curiosity and wonder.

My point is (for there must be a point) that while re-enchantment today entails fear and fascism, it also entails a newly aroused wonder about the natural world no less than its mimetic propensities, as with those frogs and dogfish swimming across the blackboard. Therein lies the basis and the hope of the mastery of non-mastery.

But in our secular times, is not the term *re-enchantment* hard to swallow? Does it not seem a bit over the top, softheaded, and downright embarrassing? Yet—and yet—is it not over the top in interesting ways? Is it not perhaps a little too polemical, this term, *re-enchantment*, chosen to challenge the crocodile tears of disenchantment?

Is not—and here I pause so as to let this sink in—is not what I am looking for here better written as "art," as when Nietzsche writes about his own work in the later preface to *The Birth of Tragedy*, where he argues furiously against a certain quality of disenchantment that "negates, judges, and damns art":

Behind this mode of thought and valuation, which must be hostile to art if it is at all genuine, I never failed to sense a *hostility to life*— a furious, vengeful antipathy to life itself: for all of life is based on semblance, art, deception, points of view, and the necessity of perspectives and error.[10]

Here re-enchantment becomes "art" evoking life and "multiple realities," which in our case today means the awakened curiosity about nature that I see as curiosity born of meltdown. By the same token, re-enchantment as art sees all of life, very much including social life and culture, as based, not only on semblance and deception, but on perspectives and error. If Realism, no less than Nietzsche's target here of Christianity, sees art as lies—and here let us think a little of Oscar Wilde's "decay of lying" as a tease not of religion but of Realism—then Nietzsche, son of pastors on both mother's and father's side, works mimetic magic by seizing on "lies" so as to metamorphose them, it being the sensitivity to "perspectives and error," as against doctrine, that provides the colored-chalk artistry of the mastery of non-mastery.

6 METAMORPHIC SUBLIMITY

The argument here is that the re-enchantment of nature amplifies the mimetic faculty, which leads to snowballing metamorphoses, as with those Temptations of Saint Anthony. In other words, mimesis has an inbuilt propensity to provoke a chain reaction in which things become other things in a process of mimetic fission, as with the example I develop below of Art/Alchemy/Politics, beginning with artist Simryn Gill becoming an oil palm tree. This I call the "metamorphic sublime."

Think of metamorphosing bacteria, fungi, and viruses, as in William Burroughs's fiction in the early 1960s, prefiguring images and stories "going viral" on the internet with all the malevolent horror therein. Premised on mimetic relays, the conceit of these early works such as *The Nova Trilogy* is that language acquires the properties of a metamorphosing virus. One variation of this was Burroughs's response to London critics of *Naked Lunch* (1959) who couldn't or wouldn't get the hang of the metamorphoses created by the strategy of the "cut-ups." Words, he said, are like animals. Cut the pages and let the animals free.[1]

That is one way of thinking of mimetic excess. More macabre instances emerge from the real-life mimesis of bugs morphing into killer versions of themselves due to their engagement with antibiotics and antifungals, creating bacteria and fungi so deadly that public health authorities and hospitals are scared to say anything for fear of causing panic. In the plant world, agribusiness mono-cropping accelerates metamorphosing plagues that spread across the globe, killing Costa Rican coffee trees, then olive trees through-out the Mediterranean countries, a nudge here and a nudge there as mimetically savvy fungi retool themselves. Products of human interventions in nature, such mimetically savvy pathogens fool not only nature but the humans who thought they would profit from the latest tool for the domination of nature. The bottom line here is that mimesis can be manipulated and used for making money but can also turn on its manipulators. In these situations, mastery of non-mastery finds a foothold.

Long before the biological revolution attempted to exploit the mi-metic faculty, mid-nineteenth-century industrial chemistry figured out how to engineer the benzene ring, discovered in coal tar, add-ing a hydrogen atom here, an oxygen atom there—a stunning ex-ample of the metamorphic sublime at work throughout the modern world. It would be hard to name an industrial product that was not in an important way the result of that mimetic engineering and the dreaming attendant on the dance of the atoms seen in trance, so the story goes, by the German chemist August Kekulé, dozing before the fire in 1865, who thereby discovered the benzene ring (which at another time appeared as a snake eating its own tail). In *Gravity's Rainbow* Pynchon, never one to miss an opportunity as regards the surreality of science, devotes pages to Kekulé's merry dance of the benzene molecule.

Around the same time that the benzene ring was formulated and mimetically manipulated in Germany, setting off the second indus-trial revolution, Friedrich Nietzsche framed much of his philosophy in terms of the conflict between the Dionysian form of imitation, on the one hand, and *ressentiment*, on the other. While Dionysian imi-tation is mimesis as an end in itself and cannot be avoided, being a love, a joy, an excitement unto sickness, as we shall see later in the orgiastic rendition of the cream separating machine in Sergei

Eisenstein's film *The Old and the New*, *ressentiment* is the calculated use of mimesis for domination, and this to such a degree that it becomes a fixed part of personhood, institutions, and the social world in general, a world saturated with dissimulation as domination. In a word, the social becomes a theater of deceit and cunning, hence the frequently heard advice from a colleague, "Watch your back," the sort of thing you could hear in the sorcery-laden villages and forests of the Putumayo region in Colombia. The devastatingly original, not to mention often cynical, microsociology of Erving Goffman is based exactly on this theater. Goffman takes this to such lengths that at times his mode of exposition—his very grammar—implodes as each phrase redoubles the cynicism of the one before, thus creating pervasive mistrust of itself as well as of the world referenced. In other words, the mode of exposition bears a mimetic relationship to its content as well as displaying the outer limits of where such cynicism leads, throttling language in excesses of dissimulating fervor.[2]

But that's the simplest and most glaringly obvious level, while the type of simulation to which I refer is mostly beyond awareness. How could society function if everyone thought it was a tissue of lies and simulations, what the sociologists referred to as role playing? We think we think in terms of rules, laws, customs, and so forth. But recall Holden Caulfield in *Catcher in the Rye* (published at roughly the time of Goffman's writing *The Presentation of the Self in Everyday Life*), for whom most everyone he knows or meets is what he calls a "phony." Or think of the frequency in professional circles, very much including university life, not only of "networking" but of the unabashed admission with which this dissimulative practice occurs as second nature. Basically it's all fraud, yet the busy bees continue in their wide-eyed enthusiasm and innocence of being, living this social contract.

As for social relations and their manipulation ("Watch your back!"), so for relationships with nature. It is my thesis that global meltdown—meaning environmental as well as political mayhem—

further augments such fireside simulacra as Kekule's vision of dancing atoms and snakes in circles consuming their tails, and does so
in good part through the ever more sophisticated manipulation of
mimesis, as with the brave new world of genetic engineering ap-
plied to human embryos and before that to plants, so-called GMOs,
paving the way for the concentration of the world's food species in
the hands of fewer than five or six companies, such as Monsanto,
sublimely metamorphed in late 2016 into Bayer for merely sixty-six
billion dollars.

Consider too the (apparently) continual improvements in surveillance and the aggressive attempts by presidents and social media to
disseminate rumor and lies in ever more pungent forms. (I say "apparently," but would we know?) It is like the arms race, but instead
of guns and bombs the buildup is now one of the metamorphic sublime, which is more powerful than guns and bombs and provokes
their actual use.

I first conceived of the metamorphic sublime as the outcome of
mimetic excess when I studied oil palm plantations in northern
Colombia with the law professor and anthropologist Juan Felipe
Garcia starting in 2008.[3] Here I encountered runaway metamorphoses involving constellations of mimeses. These were desperate
places expanding over much of Colombia, owned by corporations
and rich families that use paramilitaries to force out the peasants
living there and level the forest. One variety of oil palm, introduced
in Colombia as plague-resistant (for how long?), is known as "Hope
of America." It has a problem, however. It cannot reproduce. It
needs the helping hands of laborers inseminating it manually, imitating nature. In the photographs in the lavish catalog produced by
the Colombian federation of oil palm growers, these inseminators
are young women of color carefully guiding the procreative organ
through the spines of the palm.[4]

The oil itself is a mimetic cornucopia—a Faustian dream from which
a vast panoply of stuff can be made, from diesel fuel to an awesome

percentage of the food products on your supermarket shelves, as well as cosmetics and paints. This is a fine example of the metamorphic sublime, and we cannot but admire the clever chemists who have set nature afire like this.

That is one set of metamorphoses. Another concerns the paramilitaries whose stock in trade is massacres using power saws and machetes, reconfiguring the human body as living sculpture hung on barbed-wire fences. They are sneaky too, full of bombast one moment, slime disappearing into darkness the next. Like wraiths at twilight, they are adept at shape-changing, like killer viruses. Their phantasmatic connection to the state apparatus, up to the highest levels, is another aspect of this shape-changing wizardry. Statistics consistently show that they have killed far more people than all guerrilla groups combined, yet, as part of the metamorphic sublime, the media and the various Colombian presidents, ably backed by the US government and US advertising agencies, focus attention on the guerrilla as "narcoterrorists."

A third instantiation of metamorphic sublimity was provided by an artist friend, Simryn Gill, who showed me over the oil palm plantation near her home in Port Dixon, Malaysia, and later sent me a photograph of herself standing in a plantation with palm fronds radiating out from her upper body while she clutched a bunch of oil palm nuts to her belly.[5]

If I were to reassemble these three scenes on the blackboard like Tom the Naturalist, I would have an ur-scene of intense metamorphic sublimity organized into a horizontal sequence of three components, thus:

ART. Here you see Simryn becoming palm in a playful yet deadly serious mimesis. The magic of Becoming Palm is highlighted no less than is the vulnerability of the human body.

CHEMISTRY. Here you see a martini glass with an orange liquid, which is pretty much what I see in the catalog produced by the Colombian Oil Palm Federation.[6] The liquid is palm oil. Its color, its glass container, and its vast mimetic potential lead me to call it an elixir.

POLITICS. Here, in the third component making up my sequence of "scenes," are the paramilitaries. But you don't see them in my drawing, as they tend to be invisible. Instead, just an abbreviation (PMs) or maybe black lightning lined with red. Paramilitaries are the active quintessence of the mimetic faculty, adroit in disguise and subterfuge. I'm taking my cue from Deleuze and Guattari's notion of "the war machine" as ghostly, ambiguously within and yet also outside of law and state. Like the CIA and mercenaries the world over, and like palm oil itself, paramilitaries flit across boundaries.

This intersection of art, chemistry, and politics is bound to the bond of mimetic vigor. At first sight this triad may appear strange. That is because we seem not to have concepts that cut across nature and culture so easily, so "naturally," and so productively, which is to say with such metamorphic sublimity.

Crucial to this triptych of art, chemistry, and politics, is "art" as the trope that combines the war machine with biotechnology. Art, no less than the triptych itself, comes to life through accidents of fieldwork in different places, as I will here recount, my main focus being that of "copies chasing copies" as stimulated by sound, a particular sound at that, namely, the cry of the donkey.

I don't know if you have heard this cry? It is unearthly, full of pain and anguish. It hits the rock bottom of existence and comes back up full of renewed life-forms along with a wheezing that threatens to inhale the universe itself.

That's how I heard it in the canyons of Palestine and at night in the killing fields of the oil palm plantations of northern Colombia, "the sound of sound," the cry of a heartless world from which came all other sounds and language itself. Was it the sound of love or of war? I asked Doña Edit and young Michael, living alongside an oil palm plantation in northern Colombia. Both, they replied.[7]

It was a short step from that formulation to multiple mimeses and the metamorphic sublime, which in turn made me think of situations I had come across reading Erland Nordenskiöld and Ruben Pérez Kantule's great book, published in 1938, on the Cuna Indians of Panama and Colombia.[8] Those situations were instances of what I call "copies chasing copies," as when a shaman was called on account of a young woman's dreaming of nightly visits by a handsome man, who was thought, when she gave birth to turtle eggs, to have been a turtle spirit in disguise. People feared the island would be inundated by the sea. The authors cite instances of people with similar conditions being murdered because they represent such a threat to the community.

To deal with this spirit turtle the shaman as seer had to discern not so much the difference between reality and copy as the difference between the spirit turtle and the spirit of the handsome man. The seer's power of discernment lies in his out-doubling doubling, in out-morphing metamorphosis, as when he surrounds the patient with wooden figurines, carved as humans, and sings to them to arouse their spirit power to combat wayward spirits. It deserves mention that in Nordenskiold and Pérez's ethnography, these figurines are carved to resemble sailors from North American and European ships, but it is the wood from local trees categorized as female that is said to be the major ingredient, a stunning instance of mimesis and alterity as well as of imitative and contagious magic combined.[9]

In our performance of *The Cry of the Donkey* by Futurefarmers and myself at UC Berkeley in November 2018, metamorphic sublimity was illustrated by Amy Franceschini and Lode Vranken cutting "spirit shapes" from white paper, along with the imitation of the cry of the donkey, letting the shapes fall to the floor in cascades of copies chasing copies.

As the cut-out shapes fall and scatter, the faker-in-chief has uttered more than ten thousand lies since assuming the presidency, twelve per day, according to the *Washington Post* in April 2018. In the early morning dream state he recycles something on Fox News and then, like the birds as the sun rises, starts tweeting his copy on yet another day of rousing metamorphic sublimity. Thus copies chase copies, as do mine and Futurefarmers' and others still yet to come, propelling us far beyond the world of copies and even Benjamin's "doctrine of the similar" to that eerie world sending chills down your spine postulated by Roger Caillois in his 1935 essay on mimicry and legendary psychasthenia, in which he postulates a radical type of mimicry in which you can become anything at all, a state in which you invent spaces of which you are the convulsive possession.[10]

As for the rest of us, are we not becoming those invented spaces of which the tweeter is the convulsive possession?

Not to worry—not too much, that is—for it might be a generous space allowing us to roll over into the mastery of non-mastery chasing copies of copies while singing our songs, and although we may not have access to figurines carved as sailors out of sacred trees coded female, we do at least have literature such as that poignant mimesis of wasp and orchid in Marcel Proust's *Sodom and Gomorrah*.

Very early in the book, Baron Charlus is seized by lust on seeing, for the first time, the tailor Jupien. Here Proust spends several pages circling the theme of the mimesis at work when a wasp and an orchid copulate, or should I say "copulate." Proust is intent on drawing a parallel between sexual desire and dissimulation under the magic wand of nature's design, and it is surely not lost on us that homosexual desire, let alone its carnal realization at the time of Proust's writing, involved strenuous dissimulation too.

As regards the wasp and the orchid, the human-held folk wisdom is that the wasp is deceived into thinking that the orchid is a female wasp.[11] This begs many questions, not least of which is how do we know the wasp is misled? Don't we all love flowers? And what is it about the poetry of wasp and orchid that grabs one's attention—this sinister insect of pain mimetically engorged by a creature of mythical beauty native to faraway lands? The symbolism is overwhelming and I cannot but wonder if the overarching formula of sexual desire between insects and flowers involving dissimulation under the magic wand of nature's design is not an idea—a concept, a vision, really—that underlies all mimesis, its trickery no less than its sublimity?

Consider the frangipani.

Wikipedia tells us that frangipani flowers (which saturate the summer night air of my suburb in Sydney)

are most fragrant at night in order to lure sphinx moths to pollinate them. The flowers yield no nectar, however, and simply trick their pollinators. The moths inadvertently pollinate them by transferring pollen from flower to flower in their fruitless search for nectar.

"Simply," as in "simply trick"?

It's as if what I take to be its enchanting smell substitutes for nectar, making of the smell a chief candidate for metamorphic sublimity, which of course parallels the cry of the donkey, albeit in a different emotional register.

And there is still more mimetic trickery in store since the flower, Wikipedia tells us, takes the common name "frangipani" from a sixteenth-century Italian marquis who sold a perfume he falsely claimed came from the flower. The flower tricks the moth into leaving its pollen and the marquis tricks the market, leaving his name to mature like an old wine, bound up with an enchanting scent and, to the English-speaking ear at least, an enchanting sound, *frangipani*, inseparable from that scent.

I speak of mimetic excess. But what of mimetic delirium?

We might call this the Frangipani Effect and ask, what's going on here? Am I being led by the nose—deceived—by this heavenly scent permeating the night air, or is it truly everywhere, this mimetic skein of life, social as much as biological? Am I being led by the nose when I declare that now more than ever, along with the re-enchantment of nature, we live under the spell of a certain type of make-believe, namely the skilled revelation of skilled concealment, as when Wikipedia spills the beans on both the cunning marquis and the cunning flower, drawing together in one entry the insect-flower world and the human world of trade and trick—where Adam Smith's invisible hand clutches Karl Marx's fetish? It is hard to tell which is the more delirious, which the most fascinating, the mimesis or the trick. Am I making too much of this Frangipani Effect if I see in it the surveillance state, tweetdom, fake news, and Caillois's "just similar"? For surely both the frangipani and the wasp and the orchid present us with a marvelously cunning and marvelously stimulating amalgam of beauty and trickery, nature and culture, which is, after all, the best we can ourselves imitate from the arts of survival as mastery of non-mastery in this mimetically treacherous world.

7 RE-ENCHANTMENT OF NATURE

Karl Marx wrote memorably on "primitive accumulation" referring the reader to the African slave trade and the silver of Potosí, his idea being that something of great value had to be taken by force so as to prime the pump of capitalism before labor was commoditized and capitalism could run on its own steam, so to speak.

But the sun? Is it not the source of the original primitive accumulation? Has it not been priming all manner of pumps since before the ancestors first stirred among the lily pads in the billabongs and the sun god Ra stepped forth in ancient Egypt along with the pyramids and those massive stone shafts of crystallized sun we call obelisks?[1] Some shamans in the Amazon are said to wear quartz crystals struck by lightning around their necks. "Little suns," we could call them.

Over the years there has been much handwringing about the "disenchantment of nature." But today is not nature re-enchanted? Until yesterday it seems most of us were blind and unaware. "Nothing bores the ordinary man more than the cosmos," wrote Walter Benjamin in the 1930s.[2] My own sense is that this very word "cosmos" choked us with embarrassment. It was not just pretentious, this "cosmos" word, but a parody. Yet now it's anything but boring, our good old cosmos. Like moles emerging from underground we blink at the sun, at our new, cruel, sun. Now, the entire cosmos, from the tiniest insect to the furthest star, gives rise to a new sense of connection.

"We have lost the cosmos," wrote D. H. Lawrence around the same time that Benjamin claimed the ordinary man was bored with it. But Lawrence was hardly your "ordinary man," and he was fuming. "We and the cosmos are one," he insisted. "The cosmos is a vast living body, of which we are still parts. The sun is a great heart whose tremors run through our smallest veins." Yet despite or because of that, "the sun strengthens us no more, neither does the moon. In mystic language, the moon is black to us, and the sun is as sackcloth."[3]

That was the 1930s. Today this mystic language aligns itself not with the loss Lawrence bemoans but with its opposite: the re-enchantment of nature on account of solar malevolence. Now more than ever, so it seems to me, "the sun is a great heart whose tremors run through our smallest veins."

Like fairies and witches, pirates and hobgoblins, the lost world of cosmic fullness had been cast into childhood. In his charming 1902 home movie *A Trip to the Moon*, it was as if George Méliès would infuse the cosmos with the new magic of film. But the man in the moon had long disappeared into the fenced-off precincts of childhood, and the adult's imagination of the child's imagination was not up to the task. The cosmos was good for fairy and other tales, such as *Goodnight Moon*, and that was that. Adults could smile smugly at the child's credulity while they, the adults, enjoyed cosmic lore at one remove. Few stories have proven more popular than that of the superstition of primitive peoples terrified by the eclipse of the sun, but now all of us are about to be eclipsed.

In your face with a rush and a bang came the return of the repressed, as the Faustian pact with technology married to capital accumulation assumed its debt and the cosmos turned like a vengeful beast. This more up-to-date fairytale has spurred a deluge of rethinking about the nature of nature. What is matter? What is life? Do forests think? And so on, and on. In this maelstrom, reality itself is up for grabs.

The flood of green books, freshly minted journals, essays, research grants, talk shows, films, fellowships, political campaigns, and endless conferences on the Anthropocene, animism, life, vibrant matter, and the "ontological turn," so on and so forth, amount to a renaissance in planetary self-awareness, even if couched in crabby secular language.

Under such conditions it seems no exaggeration to speak of re-enchantment. But this time around enchantment is different. Now it's the irradiative phlegm of the negative sublime that courses through our veins.

Lawrence got it wrong because our journey through the death-space of planetary demise makes not for an absence but for a new sense of connectedness, not just new connections *but a new quality of connectedness*, first, because of the sustained malevolence of the reawakened cosmos and, second, because death highlights things not previously perceived. Emily Dickinson put it like this:

The last night that she lived
It was a common night,
Except the dying; this to us
Made nature different

We noticed smallest things,—
Things overlooked before,
By this grand light upon our minds
Italicized, as 't were.[4]

Italicized, as it were—a change ever so slight and suddenly the normal becomes abnormal, emitting strangeness, that of our selves included. Yet mine are piddling words compared with that one decisive in-drawing of breath, "italicized, as 't were," because the power therein lies with mimetic lamination, the folding back and forth that italics grant to a word or a phrase, now marked as same but different.

Confronted by the specter of planetary meltdown, I am aware not just of a connection but of a sense of connection attentive to "things overlooked" as a step toward MNM (essential, I assume, to helping us out of the present pickle), an attentive sense that includes talking to oneself as in a note I find dated Sydney, March 23, 2010:

I see it now more as a poem than a lecture, plus the making of my-thologies or rather meta-mythologies or post-mythologies bound to Walter Benjamin's idea of "reactivation of mythic force," as when he writes, "Capitalism was a natural phenomenon with which a new dream-filled sleep came over Europe, and through it a reactivation of mythic force."

Here the accent must be on the act of making new mythologies in a new language—as with the fireflies we shall meet later, little suns weaving their way ero-eratically through the darkness of the night that is this book that is not a book but a firefly moment navigating between light and dark.

Big question re the attempt to fly like this on wings of reactivated mythic force is the connection to what cinematographers call the "magic hour" at dawn and dusk, and hence with Benjamin's idea of "the dialectical image" charged with "the time of the now," where past and present coalesce with the rise and the fall of the sun.

That was a note to myself, elliptical and hesitant. But now, years later, I see it as the impulse animating my interest with the Green New Deal like that optimistic image of world history as a sunflower. By "dint of a secret heliotropism," Benjamin wrote (as Europe and his life fell apart in 1940), "so the past strives to turn towards that sun which is arising in the sky of history."[5]

This image of the sun arising in the sky of history had surfaced earlier in what came to be known as *The Arcades Project*. In the first paragraph of the convolute or file called "Dream City, Dream House," Benjamin wrote, "What follows here is an experiment in the technique of awakening. An attempt to become aware of the dialectical—the Copernican—turn of remembrance."[6]

"What follows here." Is this a reference to the work as a whole? I think it is. And of importance is the intention to knit the human body together with solar events, especially when falling asleep at night and awakening at dawn.

As for the human body, it was the world internal to it as much as external to it that was the focus of attention.

Proust had drawn attention to the internal world of the sleeping body as a landscape traversed by the sleeper. He was not talking here of dreams. His conceit was that when you sleep, you travel through yourself like an explorer or a person walking or floating through a mythic world. Yet does not the retroversion and invagination of self in self complicate things like a Moebius strip, and beautifully so? Is it not a vision in which bodies relate to one another, not atomistically, but as eviscerating pulsations of each other's otherness, my body, your body, and the body of the world?

The sunflower is a cunning metaphor, this image of sun and flower coordinated across ninety-three million miles. But still and all a metaphor. Except that this metaphor self-destructs. The notion of a "secret heliotropism" is so exquisite and strange as to convert metaphor into mimesis; I refer here not only to the grand shape of flower and sun in diurnal concord but to the fact that the words and images they convey become carnal. They burn into one's being no less than into being itself, the great yellow orb that is both sun and flower turning slow against a blue sky or, to the contrary, Van Gogh's dead sunflowers, painted not long before he committed suicide, this painter noted for his vibrating—shall we say mobile? shall we say mimetic?—landscapes, fishing boats, fruit trees, always with that southern sun burning into your eyeballs.

As with pictures, so with words. As with Van Gogh, so with Benjamin. At least in the opinion of Theodor Adorno. Emphasizing the mimetic trick at work in Benjamin's prose style, Adorno wrote that in it "thoughts press close to its object, seek to touch it, smell it, taste it and so thereby transform itself."[7]

It is a marvelous statement and to me, knowing Adorno as I do, a surprise. It sounds naïve and unguarded. Where's the mediation? you ask the master of mediation. It is marvelous because he combines this salute to "naivete" with estrangement or, in the Marxist terminology propounded by Georg Lukács, with *reification*, that specific form of thingification as fact and daemon associated with the capitalist commodity. Hence Adorno's other bon mot regarding Benjamin's "method," or is it a weakness, a weakness for the mimetic, the method of metamorphosing into a thing in order to break the catastrophic spell of things. You become one with the object, but that's only the beginning of a fairytale journey of becomings.

This is nowhere more obvious than with the absurdist, comic, surrealist, images that Georges Bataille harnesses to his own brand of mischievous mimesis, as in his essays on the sun. Here the florid anus of the ape ascends through a spoof of evolutionary time, upward through the now-erect two-legged body to burst forth as the human face, while from the crown of the head the surreal orifice of the pineal eye jerks off to the sun, the upshot being an artful deconstruction of Hegel's Spirit, expecting if not demanding dialectical closure. By contrast the idea of a "secret heliotropism" seems too smooth by far.

With such parody as Bataille's of dialectical closure we engage with the mastery of non-mastery, with its humor and entanglement with transforming bodies: ape to human, anus to face, face to sun. Was the metamorphic sublime ever so sublime? Mimesis always has this capacity to edge into sublimity, and it seems no accident that this would profoundly implicate the incandescent energies of the sun, no time more than today on account of meltdown.

Yet surely the comedies Bataille sketches of solar excess are too obstreperous and remain just that, as sketches? What the mastery of non-mastery requires, it seems to me, is a more subtle engagement with the body and the body of the world, as with Proust's struggle against habitual modes of awareness, slowing down perception—of flowers, for example, or of Mme. Swann walking in the park—into smaller and smaller parts and particles winding their way to surface strangely into consciousness; only to subside to where they do their best work, innervating our reading bodies awash in the wake of the ship that is our reading, plowing the sea where flying fish are wont to play in stunning displays of the mastery of non-mastery.

8 IN YOUR BONES YOU KNOW OTHERWISE

Are we now becoming like the soothsayers of old? Are we now becoming like ancient stargazers each night asking the heavens whys and wherefores? Do we not sense our animal selves, our plant selves, our insect selves, all of that and more as an angry sky beats down, our bodies resonant with hitherto unknown liaisons as foreign beings skid in from the unknown? Suddenly we are alive in our bodies as to stellar influence and solar wind when all goes dark once more but for fireflies, epitome of the newly animate world, reminders of chances missed, others to catch, roadside flares of pixilated consciousness.

"To speak truly," wrote Emerson, "few adult persons can see nature. Most persons do not see the sun."

But I say now that it's re-enchanted, we will become part of what we do not see, floating in the wake of Hurricane Irene and the others to come whistling up the island when all goes dark once more as people evacuate the city.

Like Marx, but a little earlier, Emerson blamed our dullness of sense on the private property system. It is a strong passage, a plea for poetry in nature as much as for poetry about nature.

"Miller owns this field," he writes, "Locke that and Manning the woodland. But none of them owns the landscape. There is a property in the horizon which no man has but he whose eye can integrate all the parts, that is the poet. This is the best part of these men's farms, yet to this their warranty-deeds give not title."[1]

But witness this notice, posted on a California college campus in 2013:

Poetry for Scientists
Meets Every Other Monday Beginning 2/4/13
6–8 PM Location TBA
To get an idea of the relation between the earth and the moon and the sun, find two friends and have the self-conscious one with lots of atmosphere be Earth and the coercive one be the Sun. And you be the Moon, if you are periodically luminous and sometimes unobservable and your inner life has petered out.[2]

Is this nothing more than the eccentric interest of the few feeding off a mix of romance and astronomy, or is it symptomatic of a growing fascination with the cosmos, both playful and serious? And what of the fusion here of poetry and science? Does this imply a new science waiting in the wings, careening off the mix of magic and science in the Renaissance and neo-astrology in a re-enchanting world?

What do you make of the tongue-in-cheek invitation? Its whimsy smuggles in the mimetic faculty: "be Earth," "be the Sun." Why do I say "smuggles"? Because the whimsy implies it's all a game, only a game—let's pretend. But really it's not a game, not in the sense of something trivial, though yes, it is a game in the sense of mimetic performance involving the human body in synchrony with sun and moon and much that comes between.

Speaking of games, are not such mimetic exercises modeling the cosmos practiced today in many kindergartens in the USA if not elsewhere? In his essay on the mimetic faculty, Benjamin pays attention to the importance of mimesis among children. He wonders about its implications for learning and wonders about the apparent disappearance of the mimetic faculty as the child grows into adulthood, or as modernity destroys tradition. Primitives make mighty mimics, wrote the young Charles Darwin after his visit to Tierra del Fuego in 1832. With the concept of "aping," the door was firmly closed on European adults sinking so low.

Today we seem a long haul from times and places where astrology aligned birth of humans with the stars, setting the child's future course. But maybe we have glimmers of such in our kindergartens, where tiny tots wheel and tumble in the dance of the stars? Are our kindergarten teachers teaching astrology, or are they teaching astronomy? Maybe both—some eerie in-between science taught via the prancing human body in relation to other prancing bodies? In any event, it is worth our while to pause and consider why the stars—the "magic of the stars"—seem today a childish affair, like *Goodbye Moon*, cordoned off for the kids, through whom adults get their vicarious moon-shot.

There seems to be a profound link between children and the stars as contrived by adults, like encouraging kids to scribble and draw with colored crayons until reality sets in at age six or so and they are made to read and write as drawing falls aside and the stars wane. (But does not the link between kids and the stars seems as necessary for the stars as for parents?)

Even if you don't recall, maybe you too were once the sun? Or the moon? Even the earth? And if so, that "once upon a time" lingers as a layer in your being. Which must be why America acted so strange during the solar eclipse of August 21, 2017. It was a burst of secular religion, a dimwitted, overly conscious effort to grasp the cosmos. Internet sites buzzed, as did front pages of newspapers, promising "complete coast to coast coverage." There were complex color diagrams of the interacting orbits of the earth, the moon, and the sun. There were dizzying maps of planet earth showing the path of the approaching "eclipse shadow" across the USA. There would be live video streaming. "You have only three minutes," advised a Citizens' Explorers group, anxious to "increase your enjoyment of this rare and beautiful event. Look out for changes in the wind and in the behavior of animals, especially birds."

There were pictures of adults smiling beatifically at puzzled children, of adults showing kids pinhole cameras and sunglasses as if explaining, if not the secrets of sex or of Santa Claus, events equally mysterious and natural to be accessed by heaps of winking ocular instruments. It was an "educational moment" in which elders would hand down the wisdom of the ages, but truth to tell, there's wasn't much of that. The secretary of the treasury flew with his wife on taxpayers' money to the "best spot" for viewing.

Neither the media nor us mere mortals knew how to act in this situation, caught as we were between a miracle and much labored diagrams of the geometry of orbiting planets. Were we suspended in the disorienting feeling that we too are cosmic beings, caught not only between astrology and astronomy but by an eclipse of our own being?

Two weeks after this eclipse I received an e-mail from an artist friend in London, Diana Policarpo, announcing an autumn equinox celebration in collaboration with Marie Kolbaeck Iversen. As the name indicates, the equinox is when night and day are the same length, something you think we would all notice, or at least be dimly aware of as the long summer days get shorter. As for myself, I am only now and again, if at all, aware of this. It seems, however, that in years past, and not so long ago, the autumn equinox was celebrated in parts of western Europe. Ritualized might be the more appropriate word, and if you were to speculate on the reasons for this ritualization and what its effects might be, you would probably end up thinking more about why the observance ceased.

Why has the equinox disappeared from much of human collective reckoning? Until now, that is, when global meltdown starts to make many of us frightened, curious, and more keenly aware of solar activity like the "primitives" of Stonehenge, ancient Rome, and "darkest Africa." Of course those celebrations of cosmic cycling were more than a "reckoning." They were like mimetic acts of mutuality, a merging of bodies, human and cosmic.

The equinox ritual related to me by Diana Policarpo now passes into the secular realm of *performance*, (as in *art*), a term to which I will return. The announcement of the event states that the evening would be centered on

the performance of magical songs inherited by the artist from her great-great-great-great-grandparents, who in 1873 were the ethnographic subjects of folklore collector Evald Tang Kristensen. The songs relate to the Southern Scandinavian shamanist culture Sejd and spring from a very different cultural source than the Protestant Christian time of their collection: They are largely (and in places explicitly) feminist, apocalyptic, anti-Christian, anti-nationalist and anti-Danish.

All of which strikes an explosive chord with the one-page finale to Walter Benjamin's "One-Way Street," an early "experimental" work" (as the saying goes), owing much to surrealism and, in my judgment, to Benjamin's study of the nature-language of baroque theater.

Called "To the Planetarium," this short text weighs the losses and gains in the change from astrology to astronomy.[3] Pivoting on what up to a few years before it was written many people would have considered extreme, if not ludicrous, Benjamin would have us picture people with intense awareness of the cosmos, an awareness involving rituals of communal trance like that of the mid-nineteenth-century people in Scandinavia with a feminist outlook as re-enacted by Diana Policarpo and Marie Kolbaeck Iversen!

Benjamin then contrasts this with cosmic indifference as a result of the ideologies of mastery over nature, against which he mobilizes every rhetorical muscle he can to plea for mastery over that mastery.

He anticipates derision, that his ideas will be deemed those of starstruck poets on moonlit nights. Not at all, he responds, such awareness "strikes again and again, and then neither nations nor generations can escape it, as was made terribly clear in the last war."[4]

The picture Benjamin presents is not, however, only one of contrasts but of their intertwinement.

Modern technology, including the technology of war, entails cosmic reference too, what I call "dark surreality," complete with its own trance or trancelike communal involvement, which Benjamin describes as "an attempt at a new and unprecedented commingling with the cosmic powers." In other words, the very denial of the human body's cosmic connectivity paves the way for its augmentation, a variant—and a terribly important one—on disenchantment/re-enchantment. This time around it is as sheer negativity, spectacular, lurid, and sublime. It is as if cosmic consciousness lay latent and suppressed but then exploded in fury as technology undertook "an immense wooing of the cosmos."[5]

Is this not also a mimetic relation, cruel and destructive as it is, turning "the bridal bed," as Benjamin puts it, "into a bloodbath"?

High-frequency currents coursed through the landscape, new constellations rose in the sky, aerial space and ocean depths thundered with propellers, and everywhere sacrificial shafts were dug in Mother Earth.[6]

There were precedents to this. Especially noteworthy was the nature-language upon which Benjamin focused in his study of baroque drama in the sixteenth and seventeenth centuries, such as we find in Calderón's *Life Is a Dream*.

By nature-language I refer not so much to language about nature as to language that appears to insinuate itself into nature and vice versa through a bewildering multitude of projections and reference points.

Looking back, I can see this was what I felt was happening when we gave our mini-talks by the beach and on the cliffs in southern California, talks that in their wayward way led to this book in your very hands, our words hurled into the wind, the surf, and the dreamy clouds, words as things caressed and straining like kites in that wind.

Let us start with the start of *Life Is a Dream* in the mouth of a gale rendering nature as the personification of human language as stormy as the storm evoked:

There, four-footed Fury, blast-
Engender'd brute, without the wit
Of brute, or mouth to match the bit
Of man—art satisfied at last?
Who, when thunder roll'd aloof,
Tow'rd the spheres of fire your ears
Pricking, and the granite kicking
Into lightning with your hoof,
Among the tempest-shatter'd crags
Shattering your luckless rider
Back into the tempest pass'd?
There then lie to starve and die[7]

And if the solar eclipse experienced in 2017 in the USA stirred the embers of ancient cosmic accord, how much more so did one of the strongest hurricanes ever experienced in the USA, arriving merely three days after that eclipse, battering the shores of Texas and flooding Houston? It had a name. Of course. It was officially named "Harvey." And two weeks after that hurricane came Hurricane Irma, pounding the Caribbean with its sights set on the city of Miami, provoking the largest evacuation in the history of Florida and, possibly, the USA. The list goes on. It seems that most US cities are in the wrong place. Houston sits on a clay flood plain that couldn't absorb the several feet of rainwater that fell. Like New Orleans it is an energy-hub built for oil, which is what got us into this mess in the first place. San Juan, capital of Puerto Rico, and indeed the entire Caribbean, colonial zone of sugar, indigo, and African slaves, is in the wrong place too, but then aren't we all in the wrong place now, except of course idyllic New Zealand, with its sheep and glaciers, where the mega-rich running from the pitchforks of the irate 99 percent are building their bunkers?

I am told that the names of hurricanes, such as Irene and Sandy, are chosen by the US National Hurricane Center, the rationale being that an identifying label makes it easier to coordinate emergency activities. But it could equally well be a Calderón *Life Is a Dream* effort to name as a mode of subordinating the fierce powers of nature to the court, whether it be a court of kings or queens or presidents. The names however are disappointingly bland. There is no political correctness here other than 50/50 parity of male/female. It's like an all-white TV soap opera from the fifties.

It would be fun to sit in on a meeting choosing these names. Perhaps the poet laureate should be invited, or a TV's script writer? Or are the names inspired intuitions on the part of a chief namer who, like a prophet, hears the name in a dream? One thing is for sure and that is the magical power of the name and of naming, as made clear by US president George W. Bush nicknaming subordinates as a way of asserting hierarchy and control. Donald Trump does the same with his naming his political enemies as a way of destroying them, names such as "Sleepy Joe," "Lyin' Hilary," and "Pochahontas." Perhaps the National Hurricane Center has the same idea of using names to destroy hurricanes?

Could it be that Anglo names are chosen for wild weather so as to foster Anglo control over cosmic mayhem originating in the Caribbean and south of the border? Or could it be a more liberal gesture, stirring the embers of cosmic kinship with humans regardless of ethnicity in the hope that now, being pals, the hurricane will call it quits?

In this regard, recall our faker-in-chief practicing sympathetic magic on TV, holding up a map of Hurricane Dorian bearing down, he said, on Alabama, and then refusing to acknowledge his error. But it was not really an error. As a king, like in a Calderón or Shakesperian universe, he is the natural counterpoint to nature, able to direct, redirect, and otherwise deal with any and everything nature can dish out.

One thing for sure is that the personification of hurricanes is what one would expect from the re-enchantment of nature when the world turns angry and you are left to contemplate raw nature face to face. As the governor of Florida sagely noted, "Once the storm starts, law enforcement cannot save you." It's just you now, just you and an angry world of wind and water.

Yet the question remains as to why the names are so innocuous and bland. Where is the American genius for advertising language? Where are those wonderful names for winds that catch the ear, names like the Santa Ana, the Sirocco, and the Mistral, names that stir the soul of poetry and, like Benjamin's Convolute K, mesh the interior of the human body with its exterior? Something seems lacking, a hesitancy in face of catastrophe to come up with the Big Idea that could do justice to the power of hurricanes. An inability to grasp the nettle.

There, four-footed Fury, blast-
Engender'd brute, without the wit
Of brute, or mouth to match the bit
Of man—art satisfied at last?

9 PLANETARIUM

Late one night in a smoky bar in post-Soviet Hungary, the lads are organizing a cosmic event, spontaneous, playful, and oh, so very slow! I refer of course to what is now a cult film, Béla Tarr and Ágnes Hranitzky's black-and-white film *Werckmeister Harmonies*, in which a ferret-faced young fellow cajoles his pals into a little make-believe, curtly correcting their mistakes until their microcosm is functioning as smoothly as a new watch.

The ferret-faced young fellow pushes a heavyset man into the center, "You are the sun. The sun does not move. That's all it does!" He gets the man to let go his beer, to hold his arms outstretched and wiggle his fingers as if emitting solar rays.

Next he grabs a tall man with a black hat and leather jacket, pushes him into position. "The earth moves around the sun," he says. The man starts to move, is then corrected, being told to spin his body while he makes his circle around the sun.

Which is about to be eclipsed, plunging us into darkness.

The camera is held low. The lighting is grayer than gray. In long shots so long that we becomes absorbed in the image while at the same time we freely associate as if on the analyst's couch. The slightly glazed and presumably somewhat drunk men, locked in that dour pessimism for which central Europe is famous, take upon themselves with all the seriousness of the world this mimicry of the cosmos and its Soviet and post-Soviet darkness.

But the ferret-faced choreographer is not finished. Not yet. Bodies are one thing. Mood is another. He speaks to the earth of boundlessness and constancy, quietude and peace, of infinite emptiness and impenetrable darkness, adding, "At first we don't notice what we are witnessing."

They survive the eclipse of the sun, light returns, a piano starts softly as the planets with their arms waving like prehistoric birds dance slowly around one another while the irate barman pushes them out into the cold of closing time.

Werckmeister Harmonies is the title. "Work-Master Harmonies," we can say, but what is being mastered and what sort of harmony?

As these shabby men in bulky clothes shuffle around, they generate an atmosphere that seems insufferably comic yet sacred too, spontaneous for sure, and something more than a game. It's not every day we knowingly enact the cosmos, but maybe things are changing in this regard?

"At first we don't notice what we are witnessing," says the serious young man directing his dancers. Is this the sensibility of knowing what not to know that we find in that other forlorn central European, Franz Kafka?

Walter Benjamin suggested that an excellent way of entering Kafka's bizarre world is to see it as a physicist might, as in Arthur Eddington's description of what it takes to enter a room in *The Nature of the Physical World*, a best-seller published in the early twentieth century. It is not only an estranging take on everyday life, but one irradiated by cosmic force:

I am standing on the threshold about to enter a room. It is a complicated business. In the first place I must shove against an atmosphere pressing with a force of fourteen pounds on every square inch of my body. I must make sure of landing on a plank travelling at twenty miles a second round the sun—a fraction of a second too early or too late, the plank would be miles away. I must do this whilst hanging from a round planet head outward, and with a wind blowing at no one knows how many miles a second through every interstice of my body. The plank has no solidity or substance. To step on it is like stepping on a swarm of flies of aether.

But in your bones you know otherwise. For we are not Eddington's scientific men, as demonstrated by the ease with which we enter rooms.

"At first we don't notice what we are witnessing."

The mimetic intelligence at work in us is simultaneously cosmic and subatomic. Our bodies conform but do not, in any conventional sense, consciously understand.

Maybe it's not the body that misperceives but the mind? Who could say? And does it matter? The fact that I have to ask whether this be body or mind indicates the problem of consciousness and the existence of some other intelligence that I call *the bodily unconscious*, and what that physiologist of shock and homeostasis, Walter B. Cannon, called "the wisdom of the body."[1]

But the most Kafkaesque thing of all is that not only are we blissfully unaware of all that the physicist describes, but that it is *necessarily* so, as any obtrusion of consciousness into this state of affairs would likely damage it, like throwing sand into the moving parts of a car engine. As that unlikely pair, Friedrich Nietzsche and David Foster Wallace, claim, the body has its own intelligence, best kept separate from those troublemakers, language and consciousness. When lobbing the ball high for the decisive serve at the end of a match with the crowd roaring, what is it that goes through the player's mind? asks Foster Wallace, himself a tennis champion and not shy about referring to great sportswomen and men as geniuses. His answer: Nothing.[2] The player is in another realm, where things talk to things.

But whether they play tennis or piano, the deeper problem and excitement for writers of the caliber of Foster Wallace and Nietzsche had to be playing the connection between language and being, between consciousness, on the one side, and the wisdom of the body, on the other.

Especially with meltdown the problem is that the body does not exist outside of its relation to the cosmos. Why is this a problem? you ask. It is a problem because the new dispensation propels bodily unconscious worlds into consciousness and vice versa. Global warming alters the boundaries between mind and matter. Knowing what not to know—as with Foster Wallace's tennis player about to play the decisive serve—*is no longer autonomous.*

As plaything of language and of consciousness, the wisdom of the body is no longer so wise. Yet at the same time, does not the broken threshold between mind and matter offer opportunities—a renaissance, if you will—for new forms of being, namely the mastery of non-mastery?

Like it or not, we are now cosmically implicated, and what I find wonderful about *Werkmeister Harmonies* is that it shows this implication as tipsy men shuffling around a bar in central Europe waving their arms with the languor of prehistoric birds. To be cosmically implicated is to be a prehistoric bird.

Which leads me to ask how come they burned Bruno at the stake but Copernicus just sailed through? For what Copernicus propounded is so counterintuitive that even today as the sun sets, so does the light of reason.

As for our prehistoric bird consciousness, who truly believes on the evidence of their senses that it is the earth that rotates and not the sun? You may know it as abstract knowledge handed down by the high priests of science who have replaced astrology with astronomy, but in your bones you know otherwise.

In your bones you know otherwise. Coming down the mountain in upstate New York at Mohonk in the spring we saw the sun setting, a red ball glowing ever redder, sinking with excruciating slowness into the blue horizon while we, wrapped in celestial fire, sank with it.

Why was that? Why is sunset the mother of all clichés, especially when the sun sinks into the sea? Is it because the diurnal rhythm marked by sunrise and sunset provides the keel to the body's sense of time and space? As a technicolor installation that sits both on the horizon and in one's being, it would seem that sunset affirms the cosmic GPS in the human body down to the cellular level. Even the mitochondria drop everything and hasten to get a good view. Cells, too, have diurnality.

In our heightened state of sunset awareness, we scrutinized every instant of the sun's descent, entering it, then standing back, then entering it again absorbed in our pre-Copernican point of view, which, more than a point of view, became actual truth, as if our sense of reality depended on this whopping mistake.

Hence the effort it took to stand there confronting the setting sun, exerting some Copernican muscle so as to defy the senses. What a flush of pleasure to project my Copernican self and align with the martyrs of science like Bruno and Galileo.

May they rest in peace.

But our efforts were in vain. In the battle of motions, if not emotions, it was the sun that had to concede defeat, while we stayed firm afoot and watched it sink in all its glory.

May it rest in peace.

Every twenty-four hours.

And now night descends. The evening star arrives. An adult tries to teach a child the names of the constellations of stars moving across the sky, for the stars still exert power, maybe not astrological power but what we call "magical," as in the children's song created in 1806, some twenty years after Schiller's famous pronouncement as to the "disenchantment of nature," a song adults sing to kids:

Twinkle twinkle little star
How I wonder what you are

It is claimed that childhood is a cultural construction, something relatively new in Western society.[3] Less attention has been paid to the function of this new child as repository of what Enlightenment trashed, what Schiller deemed "disenchantment." More than that, however, is the secret, or at least unacknowledged, pact that the adults can keep their pre-Enlightenment prejudices, their witches and fairies, talking animals and twinkling stars, by indulging children with them as if they were real, while the kids, in the main, indulge the adults and let them continue to believe at this one remove.

But amid the twinkle one would search in vain for an alternative cosmology anything like that propounded by Charles Fourier with his idea in the early nineteenth century of a torrid mimesis between the planets. The reason planet earth stank so bad and was shunned by other planets with which it formerly copulated, he opined, was because of the market economy combined with the boredom of work, hypocritical sexuality, monogamy, and venomous family life. If only sex, family, and economy were organized in accord with his model, then the earth would spring back to the sweet-smelling life of eco-eroticism. (Now there's a plan.) The socialist utopias built on his theories in the USA, such as the North American Phalanx in New Jersey, may have failed, but the Fourierist imagination of landscape's capacity to influence human society lives on in the wonders of parks designed by Frederick Law Olmsted, such as Central Park in Manhattan, Prospect Park in Brooklyn, and Von King Park in Bed-Stuy, Brooklyn, close to where I live.[4]

Fourier's expansive views of cosmic influence are welcome at our time in history when notions of "globalization" remain narrowly encased in clichés concerning the internet and capitalist trade deals. A re-enchanted view of globalization would owe a great deal to cosmologies recorded for so-called primitive and precapitalist societies in which the sun, for instance, no less than the moon and the stars, exerts continuous force in the social drama as well as in the human body.

As this point of view unfolds and you recall your days dancing the cosmos in pre-K, you might imagine even the dead enchanting the night skies, each star a dead person twinkling its heart out. That would fit with sacred geography trisecting the universe, as with Dante's *Divine Comedy*, projecting heaven, hell, and purgatory into planet earth. Strange things happen in this journey through the inferno on the way to redemption from pagan to Christian worlds and now—and now—into newly enchanted life-forms.

The divine comedy has only just begun!

Bearing in mind that the magic of the dead and the magic of stars are each a mighty force most anywhere, anytime, let me point out that something cosmic has taken the place of the cosmos, namely modern warfare, SWAT teams, drones, state surveillance, and the runaway, metamorphically sublime power of today's technology and biopower.

It should be no surprise that Ronald Reagan would refer to modern war technology as "star wars" or that Benjamin scored World War I technology in terms reminiscent of Greek mythology and did so in a language of nightmarish surrealism. Let us not forget the exaltation of the modern technology of war by the Italian Futurists. Marinetti saw "star wars" before Ronald Reagan did, but then the original *Star Wars* movie by George Lucas was founded on a mix of Edgar Rice Burroughs, author of *Tarzan of the Apes* (1912) and its many sequels, and the comic-book series *Flash Gordon*, itself based on the *Buck Rogers* comics and films begun in 1928, the year Benjamin's remarks on the planetarium were published.

What would Benjamin have made of such an assemblage, which, in the case of Lucas's 1976 novel, *Star Wars*, "unites the hardware of science fiction with the romantic fantasies of sword and sorcery," grist for the mill, surely, of *The Arcades Project*.[5]

Of course, along with heaven there has to be hell. The re-enchantment of nature due to meltdown owes much to the boiling energy of our underworlds with their ancient histories, infinitely more interesting and alive than our pastel-colored heavens. It is this energy of the underworld that I have in mind when I speak of dark surrealism and what I call the irradiative phlegm of the negative sublime, combined into a more up-to-date version of the *Divine Comedy*, as when, close to the Berlin planetarium under the S-Bahn tracks long after midnight we entered the blue glow of the turntables and saw the glowing ends of cigarettes like fireflies tracing vortices in exhalations of smoke. We rocked back and forth, taking off with the music like the ancients and those nineteenth-century antinationalist, anti-Christian, Scandinavian feminists dancing the autumn equinox.

For this was Berlin before the birth of the sun now hiding behind leaden clouds, the sidewalks littered with ice and black gravel. Now and again you sensed a sinister green and yellow effusion in the ashen sky that was the sun, like a light bulb in a refrigerator.

Yet as soon as the plane lifts off to take us across the Atlantic and we break through the clouds we enter a sunlit world of beauty and calm in which, so it seems, the laws of the universe are suspended.

The passengers draw the window shades shut.

We fly west along with my new friend, the sun. Like Zarathustra in conversation with the sun we have gone under ("as you do in the evening when you go behind the sea and still bring light to the underworld"), some in coach, others in business sipping champagne. If the passengers were, on sudden impulse, to lift the shades and see the setting sun, they would be momentarily confused, like polar bears sliding off melting icebergs. Viewing sunset from a plane speeding west is radical.

It means lifting the shade.

It means seeing the sun as never before seen in world history—while you are heading west at five hundred miles per hour at thirty-five thousand feet and minus 20 degrees Fahrenheit toward a sinking sun held steady on account of your speed and elevation. It is unnatural nature; circadian rhythm on hold where the mastery of non-mastery shows its hand.

Only the plastic ovoid frame of the plane window is there, like cupped hands in prayer providing a comforting sense of the artificial.

10 SUNSET

If today the stars blink mystery and magic, how much more is this the case with the drama of sunset? Are the stars and the setting sun relics of previously enchanted times now congealed as vulgar spectacle, survivors in a foreign world? Or could it be that they are rebooted cosmic flares, tell-tale signs of the re-enchantment of nature? In which case it should be possible, as with geologists looking at strata in a cliff face, or Freud studying hysteria, to become aware of the present as the contorted result of trauma, not only of earthquakes, ice ages, and the misadventures of childhood, but of the disenchantment of nature followed by its re-enchantment.

When we watch the sunset we do not consciously see it that way of course. Instead our reaction is predominantly aesthetic, guided by a feeling more than an idea, and one that in its obliquity seeks some sort of congress with the disappearing sun, some sort of mimetic attachment, even fusion, complicated by spasms of life-saving withdrawal.

I am aware of my faltering, intuitive steps here, not knowing how to "read" sunset along these lines, not knowing how to trace the emergence of re-enchantment out of disenchantment other than through the raw empiricism of ethnographic sketches that have come my way in recent times now that I am alerted to such things.

But first we might note how sunset confronts cosmic ennui. "Nothing bores the ordinary man more than the cosmos," said Walter Benjamin. But surely sunset stands large in the imagination since many a year and counters that boredom? What better sign of cosmic wonder than sunset?

Max Müller gave prominence to just this connection of the soul with the sun. Indeed, he thought it was the basis of religion, at least among non-Western peoples. He was a modernist anomaly, this German savant, the leading European Sanskrit scholar of his day, besotted with the sun or, rather, with their besottedness with the sun. "I look upon sunrise and sunset," he wrote, "on the daily return of day and night, on the battle between light and darkness, on the whole solar drama in all its details that is acted on every day, every month, every year, in heaven and in earth, as the principle subject of early mythology. . . . Is everything the Dawn? Is everything the Sun?"[1]

I take this battle between light and darkness as evidence of the power of anthropology, or rather of its fascination with their fascination such that now and again we suddenly become aware of how strange we are.

What do I mean?

Max Müller makes me aware of solar drama in my here-and-now. He makes me want to contest what Benjamin says about solar indifference, at least as regards sunrise and sunset. Could it be that we "ordinary men" relieve our boredom with the cosmos by celebrating these Hallmark Card moments?

Not that this is risk free. Not by a long shot. Cervantes has Don Quixote sallying forth at sunrise imagining what will be written about him:

Scarce had the ruddy-colored Phoebus begun to spread the golden tresses of his lovely hair over the vast surfaces of the earthly globe, and scarce had those poets of the grove, the pretty painted birds, tuned their little pipes, to sing their early welcomes in soft, melodious, strains to the beautiful Aurora, who, having left her jealous husband's bed, displayed her rosy graces to mortal eyes.[2]

Yet in joshing the Don, does not Cervantes re-enchant the cosmos? Is he not fighting a rearguard battle to protect sunrise by making such exaggerations look absurd and demeaning of what they purport to ennoble? Is not Cervantes trying to do away with solar rites that employ language that destroys what such rites are meant to celebrate? And what if such rites are more than a celebration in the usual sense of that word, being instead active attempts to incorporate the sun within one's being?

Put another way, sunrise and sunset disappear because they so lend themselves to clichés. It's as if putting nature into that sort of language blinds us to nature. But that too is nature, the nature of concealment that goes hand in hand with revelation.

The trick, for me at least, as with Cervantes, is to try to outmaneuver such solar conventions and strip ourselves naked, so to speak, allowing nonlinguistic or extralinguistic somatic realities have their "say."

Easier said than done.

So how can it be done?

Cervantes parodies convention by means of mimicry. He coagulates conventional sunrise discourse, so to speak, thickening it up like honeyed cough syrup to the point that it becomes painfully sweet and the reader is left wondering how on earth we could ever again describe sunrise or sunset. The parody is toxic, so toxic we

might despair of language itself, hence the allure of stripping ourselves linguistically naked.

As mimesis in overdrive, parody generates a metalevel at odds with
what it repeats. On the one hand there is the repetition, but it is a
repetition that pokes fun at what it repeats. This is one of the forms
that the mastery of non-mastery may take.

All with the straightest of straight faces, of course. Not even a hint
of consciousness as to the droll play that allows this to happen—as
with Pozzo the tramp describing sunset in *Waiting for Godot*.

**Ah yes! The night . . . An hour ago (*he looks at his watch, prosaic*)
roughly (*lyrical*) after having poured forth even since (*he hesitates,
prosaic*) say ten o'clock in the morning (*lyrical*) tirelessly torrents
of red and white light it begins to lose its effulgence, to grow pale
(*gesture of the two hands lapsing by stages*) pale, ever a little paler,
a little paler until (*dramatic pause, ample gesture of the two hands
flung wide apart*) pppfff! finished! it comes to rest. But—(*hand raised
in admonition*)—but behind this veil of gentleness and peace, night
is charging (*vibrantly*) and will burst upon us (*snaps his fingers*) pop!
like that! (*his inspiration leaves him*) just when we least expect it.
(*Silence. Gloomily.*) That's how it is on this bitch of an earth.**

Long silence.

Mimesis as parody achieves unsettling expression in theater and
cinema because mise-en-scène combines with language and sound
in coursing through the human body of the actor (and hence the
viewer), the body being itself a mimetic wonder apparatus.[3]

Beckett's enthusiasm for writing theater pieces, I assume, lay in
the "extra" that the actual body and the actual voice give to signification over and above the written word. Yet is it not in the script
itself—*as written*—that we experience the most vivid sunset-effects

because of the very juxtaposition of the words to be spoken with the scriptwriter's instructions as to how those words should be spoken?

The instructions in the script bring out and make conscious what in real life would be latent and habitual. There is, in other words, a surfacing of the bodily unconscious. It's as if Foster Wallace's tennis player suddenly became conscious of her body and outstretched racket arm as the ball falls from the sky. It's as if Nietzsche's sea creatures emerging from the water on their way to becoming human suddenly become aware of the heaviness of their bodies and consciousness provides them with a mirror.[4]

The playwright's task is an interesting one in this regard, requiring a conscious analysis of how people in general and Pozzo in particular *unthinkingly* articulate gesture and speech for maximum effect in pursuit of a desired end. To be a playwright or a theater or film director requires this alertness, which in life itself is not and *cannot* be conscious, let alone be analyzed.

To read the script is to be exposed to the surface reality of what the actor says, side by side with the reality below the surface. There is thus set up a grating awkwardness: Pozzo's monologue interrupted by parenthetical acting directions, an awkwardness matching the tramp's surly, scurrilous, blasphemous, offhand attitude toward the sunset. We are, so to speak, subject to a skilled revelation of skilled concealment, in this case stripping the Hallmark Card kitsch from the setting sun. You can hear the spoilsport growl of angry indifference in Pozzo's declamation. He is the child who exposes the secret. The question emerges, however, as to why this is scurrilous. Why are we such suckers for the sunset sublime?

If Cervantes and Beckett stage rescue operations of sunset through parody, and thereby appeal to other forms of nature writing, so can ethnographic snapshots, bearing in mind that our task is complicated by the fact that nothing is snapped more than the setting sun.

To speak of ethnography—an ethnography of people watching the sun set—is similar to writing a theater script.

In Beckett's monologue, for example, there is the stage action, and behind that, guiding the action, are the playwright's instructions. Similarly, ethnographic writing displays the theater of everyday life, its action as well as its invisible "instructions" compounded of cultural script and individual invention.

Ethnographic notebooks and diaries provide vivid source material . . . like yesterday afternoon walking in the woods two hours north of New York City, midwinter, when the days are at their shortest and the woods at their gloomiest, the sky hung low as if it were about to snow. By 4:30 it was so dark that Jon Carter and I could barely make out the trees that had fallen over the path due to an ice storm the week before. Now and again we saw almost too late their spidery branches rear at us from the ground, clawing the air with whitened fingers.

I could feel the sadness, like a weight pressing inside me, as the darkness descended, blurring my surroundings. But at the same time you can't allow it to weigh you down, and one of the ways that can be avoided is by entering into the setting sun, grasping the drama, the beauty, and the despair, all in one. This will not be the untrammeled joy of midday with blue skies and a radiant sun. It is a more complicated alchemical operation converting base metal into gold because the beauty and grandeur of sunset is larded not only with sadness but with an out-of-body sense that something is afoot. Which is why we pay attention even if we are not aware that we do so, because of the enormity of the eternal recurrence of world making, world becoming, seeping into our bodies each and every night-coming.

I am thinking of twilight as not only sad but the time to battle sadness or, better still, to learn from it by taking up the transformative properties that the mixture of sadness and dying light offer, amounting to a sense of relatedness with the world not present at other times.

Is this not the magic of the cinematographer's "magic hour" at sunrise and sunset? With Nietzsche it is often associated with water, especially the sea, while his contemporary, Fyodor Dostoevsky, writes evocatively of crossing a bridge over the river Neva in St. Petersburg as the day faded. It seemed to him that the city "at this hour of twilight resembled a fantastic, enchanted vision which in its turn would instantly vanish and waste away as vapor into the dark blue heaven." His translator understands this vision as taut with the laughter of the demonic.[5] "In that moment, writes Dostoyevsky:

I understood something which up to that time had only stirred in me, but had not as yet been fully comprehended. I saw clearly, as it were, into something new, a completely new world, unfamiliar to me and known only through some obscure hearsay, through a certain mysterious sign. I think that in those precise minutes, my real existence began.[6]

This alchemy has to be why so much is made of sunset. How many terrible poems, paintings, and sticky slabs of purple prose have gone down that maw? But how condescending it would be to scorn these efforts, which litter the record of humanity? After all, sunset is what we intuit as the meditative moment par excellence, the time for taking stock of life in its daily and eternal rhythms, whether that questioning extends to life itself, the composition of the great narrative (as with Dostoevsky), or just to fragments (as with most of us).

Well, that's one idea, I suppose, although sometimes I do believe the opposite to be the case: that the mind, overcome by cosmic emanation, goes stuporous at sunset, impelled by nothing more—and nothing less—than the vague sense that sunset is of mighty ritual import. As we gaze at it we seem to be thinking we are thinking sublimity itself.

Connected to all of this is a challenge. In *Tristes Tropiques*, for example, Claude Lévi-Strauss, aboard a ship to Brazil, bemoans his inability to record the sunset, claiming that if only he could record that in writing he would have no problem writing ethnography.

It is the challenge of the ineffable, to enter into the sun, so to speak, and practice one's chops as a writer tumbling in mimetic waves of translucence as with that other great travel writer, Patrick Leigh Fermor:

The sun had gone down but the trees and the first houses of Kampos were still glowing with the sunlight they had been storing up since dawn. It seemed to be shining from inside them with the private, interior, radiance of summer in Greece that lasts for about an hour after sundown so that the white walls and the tree trunks and the stones fade into the darkness at last like slowly expiring lamps.[7]

Islands as homes away from home make good sites for ritual and, even better, for rituals about ritual. The busy New Yorkers who flock to Fire Island on weekends during the summer, as if to disprove Benjamin's claim that collective ecstasy in relation to the cosmos has disappeared, herd together on the wharf each afternoon to drink to the setting sun. Sipping cocktails and white wine from the goodly sized bar, they gaze westward with one collective, tipsy eye, watching the sun disappear into the changing colors of the ocean. In their busy lives back in the city there is, of course, neither the time nor the occasion to indulge in such savage rites of sun worship. Paganism is reserved for offshore islands across the sparkling waters east of the big city. Islands of fire, that is.

Upstate it's a little different. There my friend Jim, a tall man built like a tree, lives with a big peace sign outside and stacks of firewood around his modest house. There is a large yard out back where, he says, he sits every day with a bottle of diet ginger ale smoking a joint to watch the sunset.

He plots the seasonal trajectory of the sun in relation to an old cedar tree in his yard. In the summer the sun sinks to one side of the tree, in winter to the other, and he tells me he gets the most wondrous color combinations, often with a lot of silver and purple. Every day late in the afternoon he sits there watching.

Surely he resembles those early sun worshippers about whom Max Müller wrote, claiming all religions come from the sun?

Except Jim sits alone.

But then how many others, like him, are also watching from their isolated vantage points, coordinating a life in relation to the cosmos in an imagined community despite being solitary? Of course sitting with your dope and ginger ale watching the sun setting is not like rituals past where people sacrificed and chanted and prayed in groups, stared at the sun and went into trance as in the Sun Dance on the prairie, round and round till they dropped with ecstatic visions, until the dance was outlawed by the US and Canadian governments. I recall once again Benjamin's commentary on his visit to the Berlin planetarium, as well as those mid-nineteenth-century Scandinavians dancing collectively to the equinox (or should I say "with" the equinox?).

Yet it should be noted that "sun worship" à la Müller is usually of the sun on high, boiling, transcendent, time of mad dogs and Englishmen, time of Nietzsche's shortest shadow obliterating the distinction between depth and appearance.[8] (Of course our impassioned Prof Müller should have very much included his fellow German, Friedrich Nietzsche. What a sun worshipper we have here!)

The sun going under is something quite different to noontime as depths deepen and reality is up for grabs while the curtain of night sets slowly onto the stage and, sitting in the dark, the audience is hushed. This is more like a funeral, the Great Adieu. Does anything grab the heart more passionately than farewell?

I sometimes think of Jim as a cosmonaut with his dreamy out-of-body demeanor, his hallucinogenic colors, his dope, his wheezing van that crawls sideways on country roads, and the big peace sign out front. He is "the Dude" in the Coen brothers' film *The Big Lebowski*, stuck and stuck beautifully in an epoch long since trashed by progress, truly in his gentleness a master of non-mastery taking in the sun every damn day, not to mention his being a living monument to the re-enchantment of nature.

Out on Long Island on a farm in Bridgehampton, a farmer named Richard Hendrickson has kept a daily log of the weather since July 1, 1930. Every day he sends his findings by phone to the National Weather Service. His weather station consists of a wooden box on tall legs holding thermometers, with a wind gauge and a rain gauge nearby, the latter doubling as a snow gauge in the winter. Volunteers like Mr. Hendrickson are important, a Weather Service meteorologist told the *New York Times*, because they fill in "the fabric of our climatology."[9]

How did this farmer, now 101 years old, get into this?

When Mr. Hendrickson was a teenager a man would come by to watch the sunset, and one day this man suggested he set up a weather station.[10]

So you see, Jim is not alone, only what he records mentally is somewhat different; the marvelous colors and where in relation to the tree the sun sets as the seasons go by. For him the sunset is cause for meditation, whereas the gist of the article on Mr. Hendrickson concerns his obsessive recording. Yet the same article quotes Mr. Hendrickson saying of the sunset, "There aren't words that can tell you the beautiful condition of the sky." Somehow this expression is more convincing than the usual poetry of sunset, and this must be because it comes from a man occupied with solar measurement, not meditation.

And yet, as Emerson said, "most persons do not see the sun."

What are we to make of this apparent contradiction?

On the one hand, the sun is nonexistent; on the other, it is over-rich. It is as if the sun practices its own artful performances of appearance and disappearances, of "skilled revelation of skilled concealment."

So too with the cinematographers' magic hour, the times at which, as the sun rises and sets, a special quality of light hollows out the visual field and transforms perceived reality. Is not magic hour magical because of its own medley of concealments and revelations?

No wonder this time is associated with the return of the dead and the emergence of spirits. That's the wonder, as when, late one afternoon, my companion breathed a sigh of relief when we crossed the Mexican border into the USA. "Why don't we call Lesley and let her know we're okay? It's getting dark, which is when my grandmother in Medellin would say, 'Que la virgen lo acompaña!'"

May the Virgin be with you!

So here is another duskland, the Virgin clutched close to her heart, spirits of the dead fluttering close by as she recalls her grandmother, while the sun disappears into the Pacific as we cross that fearsome border.

I recall my own mother at that time, drawing the curtains, saying it was the saddest time of day.

Even if our appeal to the Virgin, mother of us all, is more a shadow of a ritual gesture than anything else, there can be no doubt that that shadow is a comfort, both a comfort and a signal that at this time of day we should be on our toes generally and not only in Medellin.

This raises the question as to whether we are all sunflowers, not merely rotating with the rise and fall of the sun but existing in mimetic concord with the sun to such a degree that we melt into it and through that into our environment. In spring we feel the sun on our face and become different, sensate, newly aware of our creaturely selves. Sunbathers zone out, while in temperatures over a hundred degrees Fahrenheit you have to choose between total surrender or retreat into your body as in a suit of armor.

Such solar immersion is the subject of a three-page letter Benjamin wrote in Ibiza to his old flame, the Berlin sculptor Julia Cohn, on his birthday in 1932.[11] It is a strange document; a prose poem, a letter, and a birthday greeting from the person whose birthday it is, hallucinatory in tone and, unnervingly, written in the third person. An Ibizan poet, Vicente Valero, says it was probably written under the impact of hashish or opium.[12] He overlooks the possibility that the sun itself is narcotic.

It is 1932. Benjamin is lonely, extremely poor, and suicidal. But he doesn't write about that. On this day that is his fortieth birthday it's the sun that preoccupies him. With astonishment he recalls that entire nations—Jews, Indians, and Moors—had built schools under this sun whose strength is such as to make thinking impossible for him.

But here in the heat—walking through the heat—has he not found his own school, an intuitive, poetic, school of immersion in his surroundings? After all, this is the theorist of the urban flaneur as well as the *colporteur*, combining the montage-effects of film with those of hashish while walking the city. Only here, far from Paris or any other city, he is walking, as he says, "in the sun."

The landscape trots by in kaleidoscopic fragments. And every now and then he abruptly stops his companion with the command *tiens!* which means stop! because he has to stop and finish a thought. Must have been strange for his companion waiting there in the stillness of that hot day in that magical landscape. Waiting. Waiting. Gives you a chance to switch gears, I guess, and see things different.

Six years later, in 1940, shortly before his suicide at age forty-eight fleeing the Gestapo, Benjamin will write, as if inscribing in stone, his theses on the philosophy of history, one of which goes like this: "Thinking involves not only the flow of thoughts but their arrest as well." He wants us to imagine that the arrest makes possible what he calls a Messianic cessation of happening, or in other words, provides a chance—a revolutionary chance—in the fight for the oppressed past.[13]

Is this a spatial representation of his beloved "dialectical image"? Is he walking the dialectical image?

He stops abruptly, as does the dialectical image, when the past catapults into the present. A space opens into another reality. It is what we might call "the mimetic freeze" of a past/present overlay as with montage, thanks to the sun fusing his body with the immediate environment.

We might say that Benjamin is enacting the formal properties of the dialectical image, which is to say, he is mimetic with the image, freeing up the mimetic relays between himself and the landscape to the extent of his dissolving into the environment.

But not just formal properties are involved. Here in Ibiza he is melting with the heat into thyme and resin (the acrid smell of resin), the buzzing of a bumblebee, the widening of the path, the cold drop of sweat sliding down his body. He takes note of a charcoal kiln while the mountain, to which his gaze is drawn, cowers in the haze. He keeps walking in the sun. His shirt is slipping off, exposing him to sunburn, this man normally in a suit and tie, this "I" becoming a "he," this person becoming a thing amid things, microcosm within the macrocosm.

So he walks on. Things trade places, he says. Nothing remains, yet nothing disappears, such that

from all this activity, however, names suddenly emerge; wordlessly they enter the mind of the passerby, and as his lips shape them, he recognizes them. They come to the surface. They drift past him on the nameless distant horizon, without leaving a trace.

The names of islands that rose out of the sea like marble sculptures, of steep rocks whose craggy peaks broke up the sky, of stars that surprised him in the boats when they came on guard duty in the early darkness. The chirping of the cicadas has fallen silent; the man's thirst has vanished; the day is waning.

But today how the tables have turned! What in 1932 was a striking prefiguration of how the sun ignites animistic and mimetic potentials has now become quotidian, as the dialectical image, thanks to the re-enchantment of nature, walks us.

Whether the Messiah shows his hand is another matter, but at least, hovering in the wings, impatiently, awaits the mastery of non-mastery.

Tiens!

11 IN THE BEGINNING WAS THE FIREFLY

"Late twilight," writes Dan Torop, "but full moon. A long exposure of ten to fifteen minutes to accumulate enough fireflies, and enough light for the landscape to be seen as landscape. The fireflies form moving trails across the frame. I remember setting up the camera and opening the lens, then going down the hill and frying up some onions for dinner, then going back to check."[1]

Is this the ultimate disenchantment of the cosmos, frying onions as the gaping lens takes in a summer night in Pennsylvania, fireflies flickering around a Norman Rockwell barn, holding us closer than close to Mother Earth?

Or, to the contrary, is it a profane illumination, a mix of the sublime and the everyday, now lit up and transformed as if by a shamanic vision of phosphorescence, the night made dark as the smell of frying onions drifts across the fields?

Do not fireflies sexualize the night? Let us recall the folkloric idea that fireflies twinkle on and off so as to have sex, although people prefer to say "mate," thus evoking Darwin. Animals mate. Humans have sex. Be not deterred. Fireflies sexualize the night, rendering it turgid with flashes and sprinkles of light like confetti flickering with the rapid eye movements of dreams.

Like solar panels, fireflies store up the sun's light during the day, then release it into the night in a saucier form. Was this what Deleuze and Guattari, had in mind with their notions of "molecularity" and "deterritorialization"? And something more, that mystery, their mystery of the "plane of immanence," which, after all, permeates this tract of mine concerned with MNM. Whatever it be, this plane of immanence, I myself cannot think of a better example than these fireflies. No wonder Pasolini was so upset with their disappearance in Italy.[2] Like the unconscious of both body and mind fireflies store solar memories so as to release them in whorls and wraiths of dancing light disappearing into darkness. These tiny creatures not only befriend the dark but tease it in free-floating ecstasy, pixilating forest and field in the arcs and intricacies of mastery, the mastery of non-mastery.

They also tease the sun, that grand master now grinding us to pulp. In place of that steadfast, centralized, centralizing omnipotence so easily aligned with kings and empires (on which it never sets), them ragamuffin fireflies can't wait to get started as soon as his back is turned.

Why are they so beautiful? Is it their unpredictability, their MNM unpredictability of movement along with their silent grace like murmurant birds at sunset? *Murmuration.* The word activates the tongue, lingual ripples moving through bodies—mine, yours, and the body of the world—just as starlings in their thousands wheel and dart across the darkening sky.

The fact that fireflies, unlike those synchronized flocks, trace individual movements seems important too, as when I was surprised at midnight by a twosome flying in our bedroom upstate by the Rondout Creek. Fireflies love to stage their comings and goings along its rippling banks, flitting between tall ash trees and maples—except now the ash trees are dying on account of global warming. All of them. Every single one. Dead as a door nail. You see them flat on their backs, these giants, with their roots clawing the air. Ugly. The locals blame a beetle from China. Experts blame globalized transport. It happily chews away the inside until all that's left is a ring of bark and cortex and the tree falls. But still the dance of the fireflies continues and our hopes dance with them.

I'm anthropomorphizing, you say. But don't the fireflies stage their dances for us? It seems to me far more anthropocentric to see them as unaware and isolated from humans and other creatures than as the show-offs they be.

Let us look not only at the big picture of insects and birds and ash trees and creeks and China and so on, but let us put ourselves into that picture too. Maybe even dance a little, that MNM dance that is surely not only a concept (heaven forbid!) but a fiery flaming thing, coiling and uncoiling? After all, even a concept needs flesh and blood, its mimetic counterpart, what Fredric Jameson in his remarks on mimesis once called "the micro-narrative element of the sentence itself."[3] That's a firefly sort of thing to say. You can almost see this micro-narrativity flickering on and off as it wends its way through the forest of a paragraph, one step ahead of the beetles.

Impressed by the aesthetic and erotic power of fireflies, I am tempted to rewrite Genesis: "In the beginning was the firefly." I am also impressed by the scandal, the scandal of uselessness, and how these elements—beauty, sex, and uselessness—constitute the creekside of resistance to our woebegone world, which must be why we love fireflies as much as we love to gaze endlessly into the flames of a fire.

Is this what Pasolini had in mind in his 1975 diatribe in the daily newspaper about the disappearance of fireflies in Italy, which in his estimation began in the early 1960s?[4] In defiant language he portrays this disappearance of the fireflies as symbolic of, and indeed caused by, a new phase in Italian fascism masked by Christian Democracy, leaving people rudderless and ripe for the plucking.

Much has been made of this slight newspaper article, never more so than in 2009 with Georges Didi-Huberman's *Survivance des lucioles* (*Survival of the Fireflies*)—in which high theory is massaged to show how overestimated and misinterpreted is the demise of the fireflies. First of all was the naked fact that they could still be seen—at least in the 1980s by Didi-Huberman. Second (and who could miss this point?), his retort itself exhibited the most wondrous fireflying through—you guessed it!—Benjamin's flashes, the body-image space, and the return of the Messiah. Even if the fireflies had disappeared, they were bound to fly and flash their way through the history of ruination now upon us, as you can see from the fact that seven years before *Survival of the Fireflies* Didi-Huberman had published a fabulous work on Aby Warburg's theory of the image called *The Surviving Image.*[5]

Well, maybe Didi-Huberman has a point and Pasolini, or at least his ghost, can breathe easier such that with solar madness in the offing, I would like to consider the presence of fireflies not at the end but at the beginning of the world, as related by Ika Indians to an anthropologist, Donald Tayler, on the Sierra Nevada de Santa Marta in northern Colombia half a century ago.

The anthropologist was told that before the sun was born, fireflies provided what little light there was, 24/7, with neither darkness nor light punctuating time into night and day.[6]

From this fruitful encounter on the Sierra Nevada let me posit a three-stage scheme of world history as solar:

First, the time of the firefly.

Second, the time of the sun, with the firefly reduced to a minor role, appearing only at twilight.

And *third*, our fateful time when, with the emergence of the black sun of global meltdown, fireflies re-emerge in force, as not so much the sign of the Messiah but of something even more wonderful, namely the mastery of non-mastery. Voilà!

This last stage is tantamount to a lengthening of the magic hour, extending the peculiar light of dawn and dusk beyond its previous purview. A new reality emerges for which we have not the words, not yet anyway. There is a hollowing out of masses and solids. Silhouettes vibrate. Stillness echoes. Maybe *baroque* is the word. *Chiaroscuro*, too. Things looks different as you change your position in relation to the setting or rising sun: looking into it, standing with your back to it, and so on. Perspective becomes all-important, especially because it keeps changing as magic hour advances and shadows stalk. An all-encompassing feeling accompanies this, a non-optical bodily feeling that comes from without but alters you from within. Mood change is the mark of this reality, along with the sinuous merging of bodies, like larvae we be, dancing with mythologies concerning daybreak and sunset inherited across centuries.

Opposed to the grand cycle of night and day as much as the relentless beat of the workaday world and much else besides, firefly time is pixilated with a continuous flicker like that which fascinated Brion Gysin with his dream machine. He got the idea traveling in a bus one summer in the south of France at sunset, magic hour. "We ran through a long avenue of trees and I closed my eyes against the setting sun," he told Terry Wilson. "An overwhelming flood of intensely bright patterns in supernatural colors exploded behind my eyelids: a multidimensional kaleidoscope whirling out through space. I was swept out of time."[7]

What Gysin hit upon here was the confluence of magic hour with fireflies.

He whirled through space and was swept out of time to where the spirits of the dead emerge, which is when movies are made and the light—as Néstor Almendros says—"undergoes strange mutations."[8]

You can say that again, Néstor, master of light, master of understatement, cinematographer for Terence Malick's film *Days of Heaven*, shot entirely at magic hour amid the atmosphere's mutations.

This mutability is why we pay attention even if we are not aware of doing so because of the enormity of the eternal recurrence of world making, world becoming, seeping into our bodies each and every twilight when the fireflies return from prehistory.

If Deleuze and Guattari will be remembered for the rhizome as symbolizing a way of being and thinking, winding nomadically along planes of immanence (that's the lingo), then what of Nietzsche's effervescent, ephemeral, already nomadic, not to mention erotic, fireflies, glossed by him as "dancing stars with chaos in their hearts"? This image was unknown to me until I read Howard Caygill's recent book on resistance, in which "firefly resistance" plays a leading role.[9]

Compared with that, the sun comes across as unbearably masterful, hungry for human sacrifice in a world gone Aztec. There will be plenty of that. But I have yet to hear of people making human sacrifices to fireflies. Sorcery is more the firefly thing; you see it with those Amazonian butterflies flying in from nowhere, hovering in the steam of the cooking pot before their wings get caught in a downward spiral.

These butterflies are performing the same line of flight as the wraiths of tobacco smoke emerging from the sides of the sorcerer's mouth, floating skyward in the Orinoco where they meet the curve of the horizon.

But what then of solar sorcery, wherein the re-enchanted sun cinematizes itself, drifting with solar wind to where the mastery of non-mastery lies in wait?

"Look," says the balloonist, "You can see the edge of it. At this lati-tude the earth's shadow races across Germany at 650 miles an hour, the speed of a jet aircraft."[10]

Such solar trickery mimics the murmuration of birds (not the birds but their wheeling, darting, direction-changing collective move-ment) that comes out of nowhere at sunset to take over the city. Shadows of life, they be, fluttering with rhyme but no reason as the sun expends itself.

"Are they bats?" asked Vivian, looking across the harbor with Alex the Greek.

Blotting out the dying sun an endless flock of birds was flying east down the harbor toward the Pacific, our questions, all the mysteries, spurring them on.

Then yesterday on the other side of the harbor on the beach at dusk, walking by the Norfolk pines, spiky cruel trees that always frighten me, whipped by the salt wind coming off the sea, I could barely hear myself think because of the noise of those birds.

How hidden they were! Could the sound be coming from some-thing else? I eventually saw one bird, a small Rosella with a yellow face and green wings scrambling frantically to claw its way back up into the foliage and disappear.

How different, months later in the Arctic Circle—in the middle of winter—where it seems there is no life and certainly no sound. During the middle of the day there is a dull glow in the chalky sky. Rarely do you see the sun, and when you do, it never climbs. Instead it slides sideways, shyly, with barely a wink of recognition. There is a highway in the distance, close to the Russian border, but the snow blankets all sound except the ringing in your ears.[11]

The silence of the forest generates fairytales that personify the silent tree trunks with faces like carnival masks.

No longer is there nobody in the forest. The crowd that is the forest stirs with the mottled light of darkness arousing powers of transformation. In the city on the snowy plain there are other sorts of crowds, thin crowds, cold crowds, scurrying like lice looking for warmth in the wan daylight.

In the cemetery with snow humped over the graves, as if a new body has been laid on top of the old body, there are tall lamps every twenty feet glowing night and day. "Little suns," I call them, like the lightning-struck quartz crystals sorcerers in Amazonia reportedly wear around their necks.

By late afternoon the city birds, fragments of the solar system gone astray, fly in elliptical circles around a solitary neon light in the sky above the railway station.

Round and round they go, in unpredictable swerving forays into the far edges of darkness above the snowy fields beyond the town, beyond the cemetery with its little suns and silent humps, beyond the railway station, then back into the orbit of the false sun that is the neon light up high.

As with the fireflies in the summer fields in early evening, I follow them not with my eyes but with my heart, pure movement, it be, the movement of movement, like flames making ur-cinema. "Dancing stars with chaos in their hearts," little tricks of the trade, I call then, winks and forebodings of a re-enchanted sun in the age of meltdown.

12 THE SUN IS AN INDIAN SHAMAN

I keep wondering what it would have been like to live in "fire-fly time" before the birth of the sun in continuous twilight when there was little or no difference between people and animals. Some of the Indians, in this regard, refer only to the aggressive animals and birds, the condors, mountain lions, jaguars, and snakes. As for things being human, they single out stones—not just any stones, but the large stone outcrops and boulders that lie in the valleys, as well as the petroglyphs and small stone cairns, which are sites for offerings.[1]

A continuous twilight? Is this not the same as what I am positing for the advanced stages of global meltdown? Is this not the same as when magic hour spreads so as to occupy all day and all night? Is this not our newly re-enchanted, metamorphically sublime world, in which stones speak and animals, or at least the aggressive ones, are like humans?

No less interesting are the views as recorded in the 1950s of mestizo peasants living in the vicinity of the Ika Indians. For them, the sun is often identified with Christ, but even more commonly is understood to be an old Indian shaman walking slowly across the sky.[2] The moon is his wife, and the stars are his children.

The sun is also associated by these peasants with fire, and fire is sacred. Food is offered to the sun, although in the past fires of sacred wood were offered instead. Prayers to the sun are made the instant it appears on the horizon. I read that what people ask the sun for is justice, meaning to kill the person who has offended them.

(Here I must enter a plea. Please do not think of all this as only exotic and strange. It is certainly that. But in addition allow the strangeness to inflect your being, to refract your taken-for-granted views of the sun and of fire and light, not to mention fireflies and being awake at dawn as the sun rises above the horizon and you ask for justice. You can take this in stages. First, try to be up at dawn. That's a good corporeal beginning to reconfiguring cosmography in MNM ways.)

This fusion of God with the sun is truly an inspired hybrid, but more inspiring still, to my way of thinking, is the thought of that old shaman plodding through the heavens while at night his wife and their children irradiate the celestial vault. Why is he walking so slowly? Is it the memory of pre-solar states of being when life was not so regulated?

I wonder what effect the continuous, pixilating light of fireflies would have on one's mood and thinking? I ask this as a thought experiment, a provocation, if you will, a way of reassessing our reality today, cycling through extremes of light and dark every twenty-four hours. I also wonder if firefly lighting is what we may experience if magic hour lengthens—as I suggest is likely—with a re-enchanting nature under conditions of meltdown? Magic hour will lengthen, I assume, not in a steady, homogenous manner, but fitfully, like our changing weather patterns prone to startling discord, as when the sky turns green and yellow then dark as a storm advances during the day. In other words, magic hour is itself likely to become "magic-houred."

This is all speculation, of course, but it strikes me as urgent and intriguing to consider how the light of the world (a phrase redolent with spiritual force) is changing and how our modes of perception and our sense of becoming might change along with that.

Surely I am not one of them old-fashioned geothermal determinists who claimed that living in a specific climate and topography made you a specific sort of person—an industrious northerner as compared with a laid-back southerner, an example found the world over, it seems. I still recall the scorn poured on some poor Oxford don for arguing that witchcraft during the witch-hunting craze of the seventeenth century in western Europe had a lot to do with living in the mountains. Oh, they made mincemeat of him!

No! My interest and what I think is important is the way diurnal variation and seasonal change inform our sense of being alive without much fuss or fanfare. What has been a barely conscious and utterly banal taken-for-granted awareness of diurnality, weather, and the seasons, the stuff of conversation in the elevator—"Terrible weather, today!"—is now transforming into an alertness as when animals sense an earthquake, birds fly in circles, cattle lie down, and dogs whimper. (Now there's mimesis for you.)

Maybe I am an old-fashioned geothermal determinist?

It is this awareness that occupies the bulk of Thomas Mann's seven-hundred-page novel *The Magic Mountain*, first published in 1924, the same sensitivity that now, like a clap of thunder and the *ka-thump* of ice flows cascading into the sea, is prelude to a new human sensorium forming as the first world exits through amazon.com boxes and the undeveloped world serves as a dump for garbage.

Mann's novel, be it noted, is set in an alpine sanatorium for the dying. The sensitivity there to temperature and the seasons is a result of the immanence of death due to tuberculosis, a disease uncannily resembling what is now the new normal disease of your body, my body, and the body of the world.

When I was a medical student in the 1960s we were taught that tuberculosis was "the great imitator," in that it could present as many or all ailments. By then there was practically no tuberculosis, at least not in the "developed" world. In her 1978 book *Illness as Metaphor*, Susan Sontag suggested that cancer had taken its place as the phantom illness laid like a prolonged nightmare over society. Then came AIDS, then strange fatal viral diseases, especially among indigenous communities as in Australia. And now we have again moved on, and the phantom illness is the sickness of the planet, a sickness that causes cancer and strange fatal viruses and is itself caused by the sickness of human society fouling its nest, trapped in a toxic economic system bound to "growth" at any cost.

In this regard it cannot pass without comment that the sanatorium in Mann's novel is set in Davos in the Swiss alps, where today the world's super-rich congregate annually, at the World Economic Forum, to discuss strategies to prop up the world economy, most of which they own.

As for the body—and I very much mean the inside of the body—*The Magic Mountain* dedicates page after page to thorax, lungs, larynx, X-rays of such as treasured items, and the daily rise and fall and rise again of body temperature. It is startling to realize how aptly this applies today to the body of the planet. And no less startling to recognize the relevance of Walter Benjamin's extravagantly eccentric Convolute K, "Dream City and Dream House," in *The Arcades Project* of the 1930s with its search for correlations, or should we say "non-sensuous correspondences," between the inside of the human body and the world at large.

Bearing this in mind let us try to jiggle cosmological orthodoxy and to imagine that for us—*yes! for us!*—once the universe has gotten past the firefly stage to the solar stage of development, the arrival of night initiates a reversion to the firefly time of the Ika account, the time before time, before the sun, when stones and animals and birds become people.

In other words, now in 2020 I also have my extravagant eccentricity stoked by the creative flare of environmental catastrophe suggesting a parallel, an affinity, if you will, with Benjamin's "Messianic return," here involving a fictive past of firefly time returning as night falls today—even today, especially today, as the planet disintegrates. Could this return of the fireflies as the Messiah—of pre-solar firefly time—be the shape and motion of the mastery of non-mastery?

Continuing this thought, continuing my jiggling, searching for a pertinent image, let me ask whether the twilight time of the fireflies implies the re-emergence of a woman-centered universe? (I appreciate how strange this association may seem.) And to the extent that this is plausible, what does it teach us about mimesis and the mastery of non-mastery?

Why do I ask this? In many previously stateless societies, in Tierra del Fuego and in the Amazon forests, in the New Guinea highlands, and in indigenous Australia, to name but a few such societies as recorded by anthropologists, it seems that the fundamental shift erasing the human character of stones and birds and animals is associated in myth and story with the birth of male dominance or the birth of the sun or both. Bear in mind, however, that erasure is never complete. Repression obscures but does not eliminate. Instead it creates complexity, secrecy, and paradox.

In the Ika story from the mountains of northern Colombia it will be the birth of the sun that curtails or reduces the human quality of stones and so forth, but for the sake of my story, in search of a thought-field relevant for thinking about today's re-enchanted sun pulsing with the irradiative phlegm of the negative sacred, I wish to amalgamate accounts from different indigenous societies (as did Claude Lévi-Strauss in his four-volume *Mythologiques*).

I am, in other words, attempting to come up with my own myth, one linking current solar re-enchantment with the birth of the sun in stories from stateless societies, and I do so sensitive to the fate of the mimetic faculty and its connection to the mythical event of men killing all the adult women, as related by Selk'nam men in Tierra del Fuego in the early twentieth century to the anthropologist Martin Gusinde, to the son of a local sheep farmer, Lucas Bridges, and by elderly Selk'nam women to the anthropologist Anne Chapman.[3]

The Old Testament speaks of Adam and Eve cast into the wilderness. Freud spins tales of Oedipus. But Selk'nam came up with an even more fascinating picture of how patriarchy emerged and functions through deceit and public secrecy.

In broad strokes the story I wish to relate is this: the world, human and nonhuman, begins with and enlarges upon the arts of deceit, shot through with a decisive act of intense misogynistic violence followed by the continuing anxiety on the part of men that women will resume their earlier power over men.

Don't think of this as "over there" and "back then," as something exotically primitive. Instead stitch it into your current views and make a collage and see how you feel about your "normal."

Up until the massacre of the women, as the Selk'nam men tell it, men lived in ignorance of the fact that the spirits emerging from the women's house on special occasions were not spirits but masked mortal women who held sway over men who carried out the day-to-day tasks of food preparation and child care.

When the men found out and consequently killed the adult women, they appropriated their initiation rites. Ever since then, the energy motivating the men's rites stipulates that women must be held in ignorance of the massacre and of the powers men feel are inherent to women because otherwise women will resume power.

However, women in the post-matriarchal phase were aware that the spirits were now in fact mortal men wearing masks, but because of threats against their lives if they so much as mentioned this, the women feign ignorance. In other words, what was a secret when the women imitated the spirits became a public secret when the men took over. It became a secret known to all, involving a dizzying cocktail of deceit and counterdeceit: men miming the spirits, women miming ignorance that it was mortal men doing this, and men miming their belief that the women remained ignorant of what they were doing—all in all a great circuit of deceit and mimeses, which appears to me to create a great charge, like an electric charge, empowering the spirits themselves.[4]

Here it should be remarked that masking is not necessarily deceit. Rather, it is a conceit. There is a strategic slippage between deceit and becoming Other as entailed by mimesis. When a person paints their body and wears a mask in rite as if they are a spirit we might say they are acting in a deceitful way, but that seems crass even by Enlightenment standards, like telling an ardent Catholic that the wine at mass is not Christ's blood but a deceit.

Another and seemingly different way of putting this is that men fear women as *polluting*, a stand-in word for their alleged occult powers, especially the powers of trickery and deceit which are, after all, mighty synonyms of the mimetic faculty.

As I see the situation, this attribution of pollution as involved in trickery, deceit, and mimesis rests on the idea that in the prehistoric time of women's dominance there was a great capacity for flux in identities, involving manifold identifications and metamorphoses between humans and nonhumans. It was mimesis unbound, the birth of mimesis, we might say, in the steamy cauldron of endless becoming:

In ancient times there were already many ancestors here in our country. In those days sun and moon, stars and winds, mountains and rivers walked the earth as human beings, exactly as we do today. But at that time the women held sway everywhere.[5]

"Ancient times" here means woman's time in which the mimetic faculty, as I read the ethnography, is Dionysian in Nietzsche's sense, involving mimesis for the joy and awe of its adventure and love of its caress lined by fire. For Nietzsche, Dionysian mimicry is not a consumer choice. It is impossible to avoid. Like breathing. And it has no purpose other than itself (which is, to say the least, more than enough).[6]

The way I see it, this style and capacity for mimesis was altered radically by the male takeover. If we can term this female mimetic talent as Dionysian, then we could define the male variant that came after it as based on something like Nietzsche's idea of *ressentiment*, a culture of revenge, hate, and fear, in which a person is defined by what they are against and the mimetic faculty is weaponized, no longer enjoyed and suffered only for its own sake. If anything, *ressentiment* demands new and powerful skills of deception so as to fool the women whom, even in their degraded condition, men consider as inherently mimetically astute. Mimesis in its *ressentiment* mode is thus a mimesis sustaining mastery.

The mastery of non-mastery, therefore, has to out-mime this weaponized mode of mimesis, miming it like Cervantes or Beckett miming sunset discourse in order to convert it into its opposite.

The massacre of women culminated in the struggle between the Sun (male) and the Moon (female). Thrown into fire, her face badly burned, the woman personifying Moon managed to escape into the moon or actually become the moon in the sky, where she exists as a powerful and dangerous shaman striking fear into the hearts of all, especially the male shamans. Her scarred face not only appears at the full moon but testifies to the trauma of matricide. For the men it is the sign that they have to be vigilant. Their paranoia is boundless, fearing one day the women will revolt and take power again. For the women, who have to know what not to know, the scar is no less eloquent.

This massacre is noteworthy not only for its gender reversal of power but for the transition and merging of a person—the one who enacts Moon—with the moon itself.

In my description you can see how effortlessly I flip between a person, a personage, and the moon itself, back and forth, until there is a resting point as the woman becomes the moon. The ultimate mimetic evolution and accomplishment, we might say, was occasioned by the slaughter of the women, who passed into nature while the men exercised their newly found theatrical powers based upon public secrecy, meaning that which is known but cannot, must not, be articulated.

The mimetic transition into nature by the murdered women was, as I see it, part and parcel of the tremendous mimetic capacities women exercised before the massacre, at a time when the world was constituted as a mimetic force-field with the men as a necessary audience, bereft of mimetic talent. (Is something similar happening today, not because of the murder of women but because of meltdown?)

What matricide accomplished was a fundamental shift in this mimetic force-field.

The mimetic consequences were not a simple reversal or inversion from women's time to men's time. It seems there was a decisive shift in the operation and capacities of the mimetic faculty itself.

The nature of the world changes. Metamorphosis itself is but a shadow of its former self. Stones are now no more than stones. Condors are no more than condors. And so it goes.

But only up to a point. For the history of that other time lingers on in dreams hidden in animals and things. Repression, as I said above, is not erasure. Instead it creates secrecy and paradox—as with MNM. Based on his 1920s fieldwork, Father Martin Gusinde wrote, "Most of the women turned into animals, and one can still tell from their colors what design they were wearing at the time when the men were so completely deceived by all the women. . . . The totality of the animal kingdom, with few exceptions, was thus created in this time of the integral revolution [i.e., the massacre]."[7] Lucas Bridges, who spoke one of the indigenous languages and grew up in early twentieth-century Tierra del Fuego playing with Selk'nam kids, extended this list to include stars, mountains, lakes, trees, rocks, animals, birds, fish, insects, and yellow, red, and white clay (presumably for body painting).[8] Sixty years after Gusinde, Anne Chapman, working with two very old Selk'nam women, recorded 650 Selk'nam toponyms. One of the women told her that nearly all natural features had a mythical history.[9]

Hence it seems that mimesis, no less than secrecy, changed its character. As for secrecy, it is transformed into public secrecy with all the implications that implies for revelation and concealment as well as for the mastery of non-mastery.

What are these implications?

First, we have here two opposed but related regimes of power relevant to the mimetic faculty. With matriarchy the secret is watertight. This is one way of keeping the upper hand. With the transformation through matricide, the secret is now porous: people now know what not to know.

Second, men are continually harping on the ever-present threat of a women's revolt should the women see through the men's masking. When women ruled they had no prior layer of history in which men ruled, enacting theatrical presentations as spirit-beings. But when the men take power, the prior and secret history of women's mimesis takes center stage as anxiety on the part of men, while at the same time women are threatened with death if they express doubt as to the reality of the male-enacted spirits; it being no less important that they know nothing about the previous epoch of matriarchy.

Third, due to the massacre, nature is very much a female realm alive with the spirits of slain women. Let us pause for a moment and allow this to sink in. Brutally murdered women pass into nature. As is often the case, to the present day and even in "developed" societies, the spirits of violently killed people cannot be laid to rest and are constantly active. In this case, these spirits animate nature, in the sense of endowing it with humanlike character, and, bearing in mind the story of the moon, this can carry both a sacred and an ominous charge as I am claiming for our global likelihood today.

Fourth, a curious aspect of the detailed account provided by Gusinde is that when, as the climax of male initiation (with only male participants in the case of the Selk'nam), the mask is removed from the principal actor, revealing the spirit to be a mere mortal and a recognizable member of the community (could be your uncle, for example), the initiate's belief in the reality of the spirits and spirit world *seems to be increased*. Here we see most clearly the strategic slippage between notions of deceit and notions of becoming Other. Body paint and masking in ritual is not deceit, just as the wine in the Mass is not deceit.

Revelation through removing the mask does not destroy the secret but augments it, in line with my axiom concerning skilled revelation of skilled concealment as the fundamental basis of the trickery at the heart of shamanism, understanding "trickery" in an expanded and enthusiastically positive sense that applies as much to our Western ideas of truth and deception as to shamanism itself, not to mention the jaw-dropping Nietzschean notion that truth is deception.

In conclusion, allow me to go out on a limb even further and put indigenous Tierra del Fuego, as recorded in the early twentieth century, in conversation with what I pick up from friends such as Maria del Rosario Ferro who have lived with indigenous people on the Sierra Nevada of Colombia, and then contrast that with what I will for convenience refer to as modern Western culture.

What I wish to sketch out, again in overly broad strokes, is this: at sunset when the fireflies emerge, Moon ascends, her face scarred by fire. Night, the time of woman, brings something approaching a carnival of mimesis, a rebooting of the mimetic faculty. With dawn comes the rebirth of the sun, when what is called reality is stabilized and categories get hammered back into place for another twelve hours; stones become stones again and meekly resume their subordinate role. But at night, Moon again ascends in obeisance to a monthly rhythm mimetic with menstruation and hormonal flows.

You feel the mimetic powers released by nightfall on reading James Agee's 1930s account of white sharecroppers in Alabama. "Night was his time," wrote his collaborator, the photographer Walker Evans. The liminal scenes that knit this sprawling classic together are entitled *On the Porch*, and it is there, midway been the interior of the house and the outside world that, as night falls, you will feel the shudder of the mimetic. It is this that accounts for the extremity of Agee's text, blending hyperrealism with surrealism.

Agee pastes the sounds of words into things that come to meet his words halfway. He intended the book to be read aloud and willingly adopted the "naturalistic fallacy" that words are mimetic with what they signify. That was his polar star.

If I am even halfway right in my notion that nighttime is mimetic time or propitious to such, then the reason we fear the night is not because our vision is limited but the opposite, because we see too much. It is not only that we imagine more, but that we inhabit mimetic time and are pulled this way and that into things real and unreal, more female than male if we follow the Tierra del Fuego script I have presented.

For sure, we never put it that way—heaven forbid!—just as we don't live on a high mountain in Colombia or on an island in the archipelago of Tierra del Fuego and tell stories about the sun and women, matricide, and mimesis.

But let us imagine that having heard all this, you venture into the night. Might you too not feel the animals and stones come alive as people while you clench your flashlight and whistle a sprightly tune? Of course, today in the West, generally speaking, the only women who course the night sky are witches.

As for the devil, that Prince of Darkness, the great trickster capable of assuming all manner of guises and to whom the witches are supposedly subordinate, is he not the misogynist caricature of the mimetic principle itself?

Then there is that other nighttime.

Anne Chapman describes eleven Selk'nam kidnapped in 1899 and taken to Europe. Displayed in a cage in Paris they were kept hungry, then thrown raw meat to prove they were cannibals.[10] Not only Indians have strange rites of passage.

The Selk'nam people were at that time killed by guns and disease to the point of extinction, starting in the late nineteenth century with incursions by gold miners and sheep farmers backed by British business interests, while other Selk'nam were put in European clothes and herded by Salesian missionaries onto two sites, one of which was Dawson Island, where they sickened and most died.[11] Almost

a century later, Dawson Island was used by General Augusto Pino-
chet as a concentration camp.

Eternal return? The extermination of the women in Selk'nam mythology is strikingly echoed by the mass murder of supporters of
Salvador Allende. For seventeen years, from 1973 to the end of the
dictatorship ably sustained by Henry Kissinger, Chileans learned
that to survive you had to become expert in "knowing what not to
know." Keep your head down. Keep your mouth shut. Despite attempts after the fall of the dictatorship to reveal what had happened,
that era remained shrouded in the silence of the public secret until,
out of the blue, mid-October 2019, Chile was convulsed by massive protests aginst the current regime. It was as if those long dead
prisoners on Dawson Island and elsewhere had returned to put on
other masks, this time to withstand not only tear gas but the masks
of the regime.

13 LIGHTNING

Soul mates they be, sun and lightning. No doubt about it. Makes you think different about the sun, that's for sure. To imagine the sun held still and compressed as lightning streaking earthward is to imagine something strange and wonderful, crystallized sunlight, like the quartz crystals used by shamans in South America or those lamps glistening in the darkness of winter when the sun never shines on the graveyard in northern Finland, birds soaring over the sadder-than-sad railway station.

I get this concept of crystallized sunlight from Bataille's electrifying essay on Egyptian obelisks as petrified sun rays. The task of the obelisk is to hold time rock-still so as to empower the sun king, descendant of the sun god Ra.[1]

But today our obelisk is different. It is unstable, asymmetrical, and anything but still. It is a tree, a crippled tree hit by lightning, abject and alone. This is the body of my concern.

This is our re-enchanted sun, our dark surrealism, this wounded tree, site of wonders.

This is how Ra exists today. (Listen to Sun Ra and his Arkestra searching for an alternative future for African America on another planet.)

Giambattista Vico (1668–1744) singles out lightning as a cause of civilization—of what he calls "poetic wisdom," based on the sense humans once had, he assumes, that every aspect of the universe is animated, allowing nature to be read like a language (an idea whose time has come, you could say).[2] Vico's *Scienza Nuova* influenced Karl Marx as well as James Joyce's *Finnegan's Wake*. (Marx, Joyce, and Vico all had a dash of lightning, that's for sure.)

In the late 1930s Bataille and the Acéphale group planned to sacrifice someone by a tree hit by lightning just outside of Paris but chickened out. "On marshy soil, in the center of a forest," as Bataille puts it, "where turmoil seems to have intervened in the usual order of things, stands a tree struck by lightning. One can recognize in this tree the mute presence of that which has assumed the name of Acéphale, expressed here by these arms without a head."[3]

For Bataille there existed a parallel between sacrifice and magic hour. For my purposes this is important. And something else as well, something unexpected. And that is laughter.

In contemplating the unexpected emergence of laughter, which he saw as occasioned by sacrifice and hence the sacred, Bataille noted that the "laughter that has wholly overpowered me I remember in any case, like the sunset which continues, after nightfall, to dazzle eyes unaccustomed to darkness."

Perhaps this is not surprising if we take heed of Bataille's great love, Laure, the only female member of Acéphale, stating that expenditure, destruction, and loss have "ontological status for Bataille, being found in cosmology, meaning the sun."[4]

In this she is echoed by Annette Michaelson, quoting Bataille: "The analogy between sacrificial death by fire and solar radiance is man's response to the manifest splendor of the universe."[5] With this she wishes to emphasize the giving, the letting go, the burst of being that Bataille calls *dépense*. This is not only the basis of Bataille's

General Economics, but in the *Accursed Share* he states that solar power underpins life and provides the essential law of *dépense*. The question now becomes how would he react today when this same power underpins not life but death?

Putting his colleagues to the test, Bataille asked Roger Caillois to be a sacrificial victim so as to make a myth that would found the secret society. Caillois demurred. But times have changed and instead of sacrificing Caillois what we have is a misshapen tree struck by lightning in central Mexico fifty years ago as our sacrificial victim. The lightning dismembered the tree. It has no head. A healer called Don Lucio lived close by. He took me there. He had been struck by lightning too. The name Lucio means light.

I ask myself, why do mutilated, lightning-struck, acephalic trees offer compelling witness to our current situation? Are they holy on account of their being, like sacrificial victims, violently destroyed, in this case, by the sun in the form of lightning? Why are such trees engraved in the psyche of monumentalities? Frazer has the priest of the sacred grove of Diana walking round and round the golden bough of the sacred oak until he is killed (i.e., sacrificed) and another takes his place going round and round.

But today it seems like we are getting to the end of round and round. Nowadays it's just the tree, and even though there exists Don Lucio carrying the lightning within, the tree stands solitary in an open field, awkward, misshapen, reeking with the irradiative phlegm of the negative sublime.

In his introduction to Bataille's collected works fifty years after the aborted sacrifice at the tree struck by lightning outside Paris, Michel Foucault wrote of (the language of) transgression as "the solar inversion of satanic denial":

like a flash of lightning in the night which, from the beginning of time, gives a dense and black intensity to the night it denies . . . yet owes to the dark the stark clarity of its manifestation.[6]

That was before Foucault lost touch with Nietzschean magic. The lightning went elsewhere and social science types found their guru on more familiar terrain. It appears that Nietzsche, too, had to be sacrificed.

But let's haul back this touch and its lightning, this spiraling move-ment of transgression that, in Foucault's words, replaces the "limit of the Limitless," meaning God, with "the "limitlessness reign of the Limit," meaning sexuality after the death of God, meaning pretty much what I call the mastery of non-mastery.

No doubt about it. Language heats up when lightning streaks through the night. I try to picture Foucault, head shaven like a monk in the mountains of Mexico, which is where Nietzsche wanted to go in the hope that the fierce electrical storms would cure his fierce migraines.

In those mountains I have heard it said that if you are struck by lightning and survive you will nevertheless die if you do not find a healer whose power comes from having also been hit by lightning. If all goes according to plan, you will in turn become a healer charged with lightning, and so the mimetic chain of animate impulses continues, tying the body to the ruptured sky.

The lightning entering your body? The sun gone wild, no longer headed for a gorgeous sunset, no longer dying à la Nietzsche in the sea? Instead your body become that sea, become the death of God, a scarred tree trunk on a barren hillside?

Was Nietzsche aware of that? Was he afraid of that? Was that what he was seeking?

I see him in the volcanic mountains like Popocatépetl, ash drifting skyward, drifting through the haze of the sun where the eagle flies unblinking going down on Prometheus's liver every day because Prometheus stole the fire of the gods now consuming us all. Maybe the story goes like this. Nietzsche was right. Like the madman with his lantern in the marketplace midday proclaimed, God did not die and now our bodies have become crystalline substance, flaring in streaks of red and yellow, then catching the dying rays of light as here I sit writing a too-late experimental ethnography, emitting dying rays become lightning in our being.

As Laure pointed out, the sun got to Bataille. It is the figure of his philosophizing. The sun does more than produce excess. It *is* excess, a term with special valence and violence verging on the sacred if not its basis, which is transgression.

"I will begin with a basic fact," wrote Bataille. "The living organism, in a situation determined by the play of energy on the surface of the globe, ordinarily receives more energy than is necessary for maintaining life."[7] If that was true then, how much truer is it today, more than a half century later with meltdown, when there is a terrible abundance of excessiveness?

In this regard, the editor of the English translations of Bataille's early writing, Allan Stoekl, is wonderfully helpful when he interprets Bataille's surrealist essays as bound to a de-allegorization of the human body. But what he should have said is that they perform a de-allegorization of the human body *in relation to the sun.*

And doesn't every de-allegorization evoke another allegory? This is what we find in Bataille's sun as it rises and falls in the human body in essays such as "The Solar Anus," "Rotten Sun," "The Jesuve," "The Pineal Eye," "The Obelisk," and "Sacrificial Mutilation and the Severed Ear of Vincent Van Gogh," as well as his essays on sacrifice and Aztec religion.

Yet the truer and more original surreality lies with our current reality. No need for pineal eyes jerking off to the sun from the crowns of our heads and so forth. Just look around you as the world gets angrier and crazier, like a certain whaling captain out of Nantucket name of Ahab, a solar jigsaw puzzle of mysterious incandescence. He "looked like a man cut away from the stake," says Ishmael, "when the fire has overrunningly wasted all the limbs without consuming them." There was a "lividly whitish" scar running down his face and neck, in fact his entire body, like "that perpendicular seam sometimes made in the straight, lofty trunk of a great tree, when the upper lightning tearingly darts down it."[8]

(You see? Our acephalic lightning-struck tree was there all the time, waiting its turn.)

What manner of "overrunningly wasted" man is this who dedicates his life and those of his crew to capturing and killing the white whale no matter how much ocean they cross?

Two things make such a man: first, the fabulous white whale, Moby Dick, who tore off his leg, now replaced by a white leg of whalebone; and second, his being seized by lightning, which will strike again, sparking fire on the masts of the ship in what Ishmael calls a "lofty, tri-pointed trinity of flames."

With his foot upon a Parsi sailor, Ahab calls down upon himself these flames. The Parsi sailor is a fire-worshipping follower of Zoroaster, about whom Nietzsche modeled an entire book, *Thus Spoke Zarathustra*.

Nietzsche's sunsets have the sun disappearing into the sea, like Ahab's scar running the length of his body, recalling a tree cleft by lightning. "Oh, thou clear spirit," Ahab says to the lightning, "of thy fire thou madest me, and like a true child of fire, I breathe it back to thee."[9] This we call a mimetic relationship no less than a reciprocating gift relationship.

Ahab was a mimetic man, for sure, a Bataillian obelisk of petrified sun rays. It had gotten rough, that embrace with the white whale. He lost a leg but gained a cause, but that's way too mild a term for the sacred surge within.

The new leg was of whalebone, as if this physical connection, like sympathetic magic, took him ever closer to his prey until he became the prey of his prey.

He talked with lightning, which is to say with the spirit of lightning. Frightening talk, full of fury. "A true child of fire," he says, meaning lightning, his foot on the fireman as flames dance on the masts. "I breathe it back to thee."

The man has become lightning.

But what of the whale with that oddly unfamiliar name, our Moby Dick? What has he become gliding through the depths other than the phantasmatic specter of the metamorphic sublime?

14 IS MAGIC DOMINATION OF NATURE?

As things heat up do not the eyes, in the words of the young Marx and Engels, "become their own theoreticians," not because of what they called "communism," but because of global meltdown?[1]

It was an intriguing idea, for sure, that not only does the political economic environment determine our mode of perception but the sense organs, thanks to communism, meaning the abolition of private property, will themselves think and theorize because of new circuits connecting mind and matter, insides with outsides, circuits that transform these very distinctions.

So what happens if instead of communism we substitute our current meltdown, and what might that imply for magic as domination versus magic as mastery of non-mastery?

Today a considered appraisal of this question would, I think, inquire into the gift economy rather than "communism" and connect the gift to the mimetic faculty, for is not mimesis itself a profound expression of the gift with its obligation to reciprocate?

Does not the very idea of sympathetic magic offer a striking example of the gift principle mediated by mimesis? Sympathetic magic comes from making a copy in ritual of that which is to be affected, and this has a twofold dynamic. First, the ritually fabricated copy acquires power simply by being a copy, and second, this power affects what the copy is a copy of. Mimesis is thus not replication. We could say it is repetition with a difference and note that it is this, being the same and being different, that is magical, not in a conceptual logic sort of way but in the materiality and sensuality of the items hovering in their medley of connectednesses.

It is crucial to bear in mind that the copy may be far from exact and that in magical worlds copies can be "fake," as with what we call "spin." You can see this with the president tweeting early in the morning, a powder keg of sympathetic magic, or on TV with his black marker pen adjusting the path of Hurricane Dorian so it sweeps off track into Alabama. After all, weather magic is as old as the hills.

The other branch of sympathetic magic, namely "contagious magic," works through a part-whole relationship involving an actual, physical connection with what is to be affected—for instance, a person's clothing, fingernails, feces, blood, hair, or sexual emissions. (In Jacobson's linguistic theory this is the "metonymic" contrast to the "metaphoric" pole of signification as likeness.)

In either case, or both together, magic or energy, or whatever the word is, comes from the curious relationship set up between the two entities, original and copy, and this we can also call reciprocation, meaning a gift relationship.

Likewise, in modern Western society no less than non-Western, just as sympathetic magic rests on the gift principle operating back and forth between images, things, and people, in any combination, so does mimesis rest on the gift as that which obliges return.

If thereby we see mimesis as gift exchange, we also see how mimesis dissolves persons into that which is exchanged in metamorphic back-and-forth reciprocities of personhood. To adopt Benjamin's formulation of the mimetic faculty, one becomes Other, in this case meaning the thing or image exchanged, as when a child "becomes" the windmill being mimicked. These are transient moments of becoming and un-becoming. We meet the Other in soulful hybridity, enlarged thus in our beingness, then dissolve back into altered patterns of difference. Ad infinitum. It is a game we play continuously. We call it life. Yet that life depends upon the intricacies and intimacies of that "soulful hybridity," on whether it be motivated by the magic of dominance or by something even more complex summed up as the mastery of non-mastery.

With regard to gifts, let us consider the magic in Malinowski's 1922 description of the Kula Ring and Kula valuables, a cycle of gift exchanges in the Trobriand Islands in which color and scent and poetry are expended along with the life-force of the human recipient and the donor.

And there is also magic, but of a different sort, in Trobriand gardening, in which earth and yams are brought into each other's orbit, nay, into each other's being, through chains of mimetic relays involving scent, shape, color, gesture, and song. It seems to me here obvious that magic, gift, and mimesis are conjoined, understanding the mimeses in question as pertaining not merely to the human performance of magic but to the performances undertaken by plants and soil themselves.

In his "Digression on Magical Ingredients," which he fears might be too tedious for his readers, Malinowski cites the following ingredients, among others, as necessary for a healthy garden and a good crop of yams:

First are the coconut leaves which are dark green which is what the garden yams should be if they are to be strong and healthy.

Second, the leaf of the *areca* nut "used for exactly the same reason."

Third, *Ge'u*, "the native name for enormous mounds scraped together by a bush-hen for brooding purposes." A chunk is dug out, taken to the garden where it is crumbled in one's fingers in the hope that just as the mound is large, so the yams shall grow and swell up.

Fourth, chalk is scraped off large mounds of coral known as *kaybu'a*, which refers to their massive and spherical shape which is the proper shape for the maturing *yam*.

Fifth, *Kabwabu* are large round nests that hornets make in the ground. The yam should be as bulging and as round as these nests.

These magical ingredients refer to color, shape, and size. But beauty and scent are just as important.

Ubwara is a small bush plant with long white tubers that the natives say are white and beautiful to look at. It is used in the hope that the yam shall also be white and beautiful.

White petals of an especially fragrant pandanus are used partially because of their scent and partially in the hope that the yams will be as thick and as large and as long as the aerial roots of the pandanus.[2]

The list continues. But you get the idea, the mimetic idea, that quite apart from if not downright opposed to the received anthropological and other wisdoms regarding metaphors, similes, symbols, and analogies, the magic here is a mimetic magic taking advantage of the mimetic faculty in both plants and humans. Indeed, all of these terms (metaphor, symbol, and analogy) are built on unacknowledged mimetic proclivities and activity.

Yet I cannot but think that there is something disappointing in these lists and that there is reason for Malinowski fearing them to be tedious. For all his vaunted linguistic prowess and evocative skill as a writer, the items listed come across as blunt and banal, relieved of any and all performative flurry or poetic resonance, which is to say of any profound meaning and emotion.

But then there is that extraordinary mimetic organ, the human voice, in this case the voice of the garden magician whispering spells into what Malinowski calls the "magical prisms" of lofty pole structures built for each garden plot. The spell repeats the word, *anchoring*. This refers to the hope of anchoring the tubers deep and securely in the soil. Each conceivable item in the "magical prism" of poles and in the immediate surroundings is named, thus

My *tula*, my partition stick, shall be anchored
My *yeye'i*, my slender support, shall be anchored
My *kaivalil*, my great yam pole, is anchored
Etc etc
It is anchored, my garden is anchored
Like an immovable stone in my garden
Like the bed-rock in my garden
Etc, etc[3]

The meaning of the word *anchoring* is one thing, an imitative thing; the insistent naming of the many different elements is another; and the studied repetition of that one word, *anchoring*, is still another. The repetition seems to me to be like a hypnotic trance percolated into the garden via the "magical prism," the sound as pure sound full of force along with the very being of the magician via his breathing presence into things.

Naming seems especially important here. Naming of things. One after the other. As if plucked from real life so as to be nourished and cherished in their newfound linguistic echo chamber of magnifying mimesis. The name establishes the mimetic link between utterance and thing. (Think back to previous pages discussing the naming of hurricanes by the US government.)

Aesthetics, too. Aesthetics as key. Malinowski is always fighting this rearguard action against utilitarianism. In his gardens, meaning Trobriand gardens, the beauty of the rites and the beauty of the "magical prisms" is paramount and decisive, beauty "for its own sake," as he says.[4]

All of which brings us to the question of beauty in the domination of nature: Is it a means or an end? Or both?

Horkheimer and Adorno's *Dialectic of Enlightenment* can be read as strategically ambiguous with regards to shamanism and magic in the domination of nature. Sometimes magic is derided as pseudoscience and shamans seen as grifters. Other times shamanism provides a foil to enlightenment endeavor. At still other times, enlightenment itself is seen as magic disguised as science. But nowhere is there an appreciation of magic as art, although decades later the bulky tome that is *Aesthetic Theory* was rolled out by Adorno, basically a surreptitious love fest with mimesis as the guiding light of aesthetics, as if the very word, "mimesis," were nothing less than a magical hieroglyph.

I think we can get an idea of the place of art in the magic of modern technology and the domination of nature by considering Sergei Eisenstein's 1929 film *The General Line*, also known as *The Old and the New*, which juxtaposes traditional magic with technology revved up by Bolshevik dreams.

In one sequence an Orthodox priest leads the starving villagers through the dry fields beseeching the heavens for rain. A cloud appears. Incense wafts. The cloud moves across the sky. But no rain. The peasants kneel and beat upon the earth. Icons and banners shake with emotion.

Eyes roll.

Still no rain.

Cut.

Now we see the commissar bringing a shiny new machine to the recently established village cooperative. Like a magician he unveils it in front of the peasants. The machine is a cream separator for making butter. A woman pours in milk, and a young man vigorously turns the handle, faster and faster.

Nothing happens.

The peasants are skeptical. Eyes roll exactly, mimetically, like in the previous scene of the religious procession. The peasants smirk, sullen and suspicious until, with infinite slowness, drops of cream appear at the mouth of the shiny spout, and before we are aware the room is sprayed with droplets of cream splattering the faces of the now smiling skeptics. In some shots, the screen in its entirety is covered with arcs and flows of cream.

So, here are two types of mimesis aimed at dominating nature, one religious, the other scientific, one traditional, the other modern.

Mimetic art flows copiously in both, and to cap it off, splendidly, each scene is a mimetic replica of the other—with the enormous difference that the miracle occurs not with the priest but with the commissar.

What's more, the decisive presence of magic in the milk separator sequence is unstated so as to separate it from the priest beseeching the heavens for rain. Religion is magic. No doubt about it. Magical and outdated. Rubbish, to be scorned by the audience, while the milk separator is coded as technical and scientific—but also as art as in the marvelous extravagance of the cum shot and art also as in the wonders of engineering and science.

Here's the question: is the cream separator sequence any less magical than the priest praying for rain? Certainly it is presented as a miracle, even though Bolshevik theology disallows miracles in favor of muscles and machines. The young man rotates the handle vigorously, wheels engage, the centrifuge spins, and when the demonstration succeeds, the skeptical faces are covered with smiles as well as with cream. What is the difference from a magician pulling a rabbit out of a hat? Sure, you can have your cake and eat it, your magic as well as your science.

While the priest and his pathetic flock present ritual in high gear, with chanting and incense and extravagant bodily movements (the peasants' supplication, the priest's fierce uprightness), the commissar has no less a ritual—the ritual of the modern, the ritual of technology, the ritual of the Bolshevik revolution—all of which Eisenstein achieves fulsomely through inspired erotic reference.

The priest talks to God in his language of chant and prayer as the incense wafts heavenward and the faces of the villagers burst with longing and mute despair. The machine in its sheen conveys the luster of the revolution. What's more, the machine cunningly inserts itself into nature, into the physical properties of milk as fat and water and, mimicking the butter-churning craft of women since millennia, spins the milk at high speed until the cream separates. Most miraculous of all is the translation between the human body rhythmically rotating the wheel and the cream separating from the milk to spurt heavenward. Is this not what Benjamin would call a "non-sensuous correspondence" or, better still, what I call a "mimetic relay"? Divine, it be. In this competition between the rain-making priest and the cream separator spouting cream like rain, the latter wins hands down, but only because Eisenstein brings out the magic in the machine.

Please note that mimesis exists no less in the actual events than in their depiction, in the reality as much as in its representation.

The depiction exposes and brings out the mimesis inherent in the events and does so by means of the mimesis of mimesis. You feel in your own body the aching despair of the peasants crawling on the ground beneath a cloudless sky. When the priest rolls his eyes, the whites glaring at you like headlights on a summer's day, he is signaling his awareness of the tricks he is pulling; it's as if he is winking at you, which makes you an accomplice in his trickery and (at least some of) the mysteries of religion. As for the mimetic efflorescence of the cream separator reaching climax, is it not utterly charming, as when we speak, in English at least, of a magical charm?

While both events are aimed at altering nature (making rain and making butter), this ostensibly propagandistic film veers off script into art as enjoyment and, be it noted, the mimetic thrill of imitation as only silent film can do to perfection. Does this enjoyment enhance the propaganda, or does it shed propaganda in favor of the original dreams and hopes of the revolution?

That would be the Eisenstein touch, we could say, reflecting the dilemma of making art under zealous state auspices. In the one moment we have both mastery and the countermove, mastery of non-mastery, and it is this deflection, this Eisensteinian sabotage, this wink of the high priest of cinema, bringing not rain but not only mimesis that construes the bridge between the modern technology of filmmaking, rain magic, and butter-making magic, but the wink that is, as Barthes would instruct, the mastery of non-mastery. Voila!

15 THE ALPHA AND OMEGA OF ALL MASTERY

Mastery of non-mastery is a shamanic conjuring with the bodily unconscious, a variant of which is called "proprioception" whereby without you knowing it, your body unthinkingly adjusts to space. It is as if you are actually part of the rooms and hallways, open skies and fields, streets and subway tunnels you pass through. Of course, our fierce individualism struggles against such leakage of our favorite possession, namely ourselves, into our environs, and we consciously object to becoming part of larger wholes, including the realms of the spirits of the dead.

Recall how after a few days and especially nights you become accustomed to, or at least proprioceptively attuned to, a new living space. You become part of it as it becomes part of you. Proust experiences exquisite agony when having to sleep in a new space on account of the time required to make this adjustment, but then he is proprioceptively hypersensitive, that's for sure.

Proprioception is a strange word in that it refers to something everyday but nevertheless strange. We sort of get what it means, but not really. It slips past like a wraith. It is as if it knows us better than we know it.

Proprioception includes your relationship to large objects, chairs, tables, beds, doorways, empty hallways, and crowded restaurants.

The list is endless. *It is as if objects communicate with you as well as with one another.* In his essay on mimicry, Roger Caillois went so far as to speak of seduction, meaning seduction of people by space.[1]

This is strange. Even stranger is how we take this capacity for granted. But then, we have to.

I became aware of this on seeing rows of haystacks from a moving train in northern France. For the life of me they were communicating with each other, things talking to things, all the more real, all the more poignant, on account of my speeding past them on steel rails, and me being not a haystack but a human, privy to their intercourse. I hear the rails hum as I write this, and I hear the haystacks yawning like in a *New Yorker* cartoon, "Here comes the 5:34." Of course, being French haystacks they would say the 17:34.

If cartoons tickle the bodily unconscious, making us aware of what we didn't know we knew, what of the ethnographer's notebook and its sketches that I present here?

You see the haystacks.

They see you.

Sympathetic magic, you say. For sure. The haystacks are doing magic, making a copy of me. Is that the secret of proprioception?

In any case, note the inexactitude—the strategic inexactitude—of the copy. Not perfect replicas. Not Courbet haystacks heavy with the sweat of labor. But yellowish circles in rows and columns. Had to be that way. A fast train and a fast sketcher. A momentary impression in a fast world. And you thought haystacks were solo and stiller than still?

Drawings in ethnographic notebooks provide an express ride to the bodily unconscious. Visual imagery skirts around words, and yet is

HAY STACKS FROM THE TRAIN WINDOW

Hay stacks a la moderne
("things do things do things") drawn
from
train Paris — Brittany
18th August
may back to

Paris

20th August, Brooklyn — 6:00 Am —
left v. suddenly yesterday, Helene

enhanced by the combination of words and picture. Such notebooks are the epitome of the provisional, one step ahead of the grave that is the finished book or the finished painting.

As for haystacks, so for the curvature of the earth. When Othmar H. Ammann designed the 4,259-foot span of the Verrazano-Narrows Bridge in 1959, he calculated that the Brooklyn and Staten Island towers would be one and five-eighths inches further apart at their summits than at their bases, because of the curvature of the earth.[2]

This shakes me up because of (1) having to take the curvature of the earth consciously into account makes me suddenly become aware of the roundness of the planet on which I stroll and (2) the enormous discrepancies in sizes involved: one and five-eighths inches compared to 4,259 feet.

But that doesn't shake me up as much as when I read of the iron-worker who helped build the top of 1 World Trade Center: "I look south I see the towers of the Verrazano and I remember my grandfather Gene Spratt built that bridge. And if I turn north I see the Penn Central building across from Madison Square Garden. That's my dad's building."[3]

I am shaken up because of the enormous discrepancy between what these workers build and "own" ("that's my dad's building") as compared with the legal owners, who by comparison stand at one and five-eighths of an inch.

Being shaken by this is but prelude to the mastery of non-mastery, because all of a sudden "ownership" is transferred from people with money to people emerging from mythology who walk on beams sixty stories off the ground and build stuff. Both dominate nature, the one with capital—the ultimate mimetic flux—the other with bodily skill and an intimate knowledge of building at the service of capital.

Balancing on a girder sixty stories up building stuff is no less magical than the story told Walter Benjamin by the famous juggler Rastelli concerning another famous juggler long ago whose act consisted in having a large ball dance to his flute music around every part of his body and eventually come to rest on his finger "like a little bird."[4]

Perhaps Rastelli was talking about himself? After all, he was supposed to be the greatest juggler of all time, capable of juggling ten balls at once (you can see him on YouTube). Perhaps Benjamin is conjuring too, playing with us? There is some juggling going on with this nicely paced story, for sure, just as there was, believe it or not, a dwarf hidden inside the ball manipulating compression springs to make the trick work.

The juggler accepted an invitation from the sultan in Constantinople, famous as much for cruelty as for generosity. The act proceeded beautifully with the ball finally leaping onto the juggler's finger. Not an opportunity is missed in this tale to focus our attention on the juggler, repeatedly referred to as "the master."

As for the ball, it has become the master's "living partner." Like our haystacks it has lost the inertia of objecthood. Not only has it become lively, but its mood and behavior keep changing, "now docile, now obstinate, now affectionate, now mocking, now obliging, now dilatory."

More than a story about juggling, you could say this is a lesson in proprioception, wherein objects become like people or, more accurately, objects and people manifest their companionship.

But here's what happened.

On his way back to his lodging the juggler received a note:

Dear Master, you must not be angry with me. Today you cannot appear before the sultan. I am sick and cannot leave my bed.[5]

In other words, in case you missed this sleight of hand, *the trick worked without the trick.*

Some other trick came into play.

This tale presents "the alpha and omega of all mastery," writes Benjamin, in which the "hand has, so to speak, taken the matter in hand and has joined forces with the object."

That the juggler has spent years practicing, he goes on to say, "does not mean that either his body or the ball is 'in his power,' but it enables the two to reach an understanding behind his back . . . this is what is called 'practice.' It is successful because the will abdicates its power once and for all inside the body, abdicates in favor of the organs—the hand, for instance."[6]

Is not this story a marvelous enactment of the skilled revelation of skilled concealment, an enactment that cannot stop, revealing more and concealing more at each turn?

And is it not equally marvelous in its mastery of non-mastery, abjuring power as "the two reach an understanding behind his back" (where the bodily unconscious best functions)? As for marvels, let us note (1) the marvel of juggling so miraculous that the juggler's hands do not even touch the bouncing ball, which responds, however, to his flute playing; (2) the revelation that inside the ball is a dwarf; (3) the further revelation that on this occasion, the act succeeded despite the dwarf's absence, such that (4) a further secret is enshrined, namely the mystery of proprioceptive practice, a wisdom of the body that ensures an unconscious or largely unconscious bond between juggler and ball. This is "an understanding behind his back."

Here we have it: the mastery of non-mastery conjuring with the bodily unconscious that all good tricks require. The sultan is tricked; the ball is tricked; the juggler is tricked; and we are like the dwarf hidden in the ball except for this one performance. We recipients of the story are the only ones not tricked by the trick, but we are tricked in another way where trickery leads to mystery, as in that tongue-stretching mouthful, *pro-pri-o-cep-tion*, a word looking for a meaning. Only a famous juggler could tell this story and get away with it, for it is a story that both reveals and conceals trickery itself.

What are we to make of the fact that the dwarf crops up again five years later in Benjamin's "Theses on the Philosophy of History," which begins by drawing a parallel between Marxist revolution and an eighteenth-century chess-playing automaton dressed in so-called Turkish attire. (One commentator describes the costume as that of an "oriental sorcerer."[7]) Beneath the chess table is hidden a hunchbacked dwarf, a chess master who actually makes the moves. The automaton thereby wins every match. Some people said the dwarf was in fact a Russian cavalry officer who had lost his legs in battle. Speculation was rife.

This dwarf is theology, says Benjamin, but theology is now wizened and out of sight.

But with this dwarf, he says, Marxism would triumph.

I can't help thinking that Benjamin leads us somewhat astray with this word, "theology." He should have said "magic," as in the magic of the conjuror, or for that matter, "shamanism." As for theology here, is not the fact that it is wizened and out of sight, a replay of Rastelli's dwarf?

Another interpretation of this automaton Turk with its concealed dwarf is that it fairly represents and replicates orthodox Marxism; that orthodox Marxism is in fact a concealed religious and magical practice (which like the dwarf cannot be admitted), making of Marxism a consequential twentieth-century shamanic act of skilled revelation of skilled concealment.

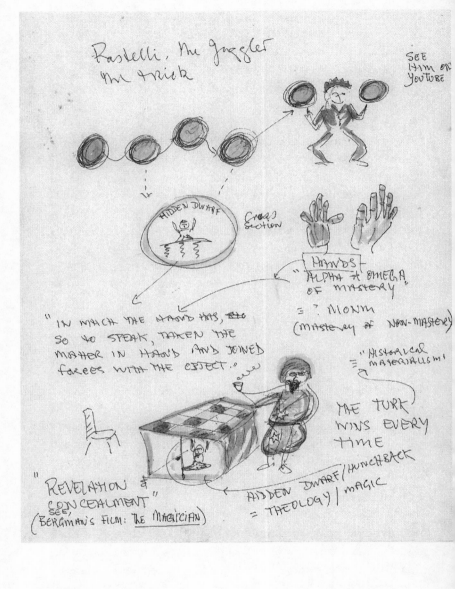

Rastelli, the juggler
the trick

SEE HIM ON YOUTUBE

HIDDEN DWARF

cross section

HANDS
"ALPHA & OMEGA OF MASTERY"

= ? MONM
(MASTERY OF NON-MASTERY)

"IN WHICH THE HAND HAS, so to SPEAK, TAKEN THE MATTER IN HAND AND JOINED FORCES WITH THE OBJECT."

"HISTORICAL MATERIALISM"

THE TURK WINS EVERY TIME

"REVELATION & CONCEALMENT"
SEE,
(BERGMAN'S FILM: The MAGICIAN)

HIDDEN DWARF/HUNCHBACK
= THEOLOGY / MAGIC

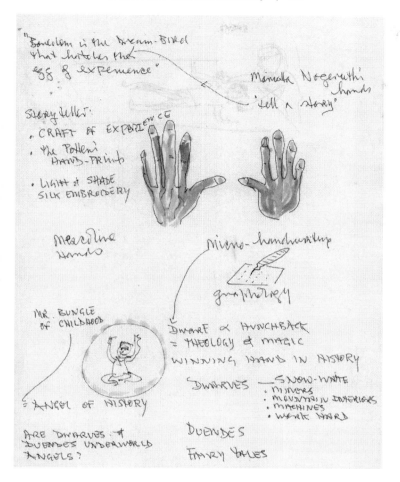

One of the most ingenious things about the chess-playing automaton trick (or *simulacrum, dissimulation, mimesis*) is that it includes a sort of game, a seduction, by means of concealment and revelation. For beneath the Turk, where the dwarf was hidden, were multiple doors and compartments, such that curious onlookers could peer into the cabinet from all sides and see it as empty. This is similar to the time-honored gesture of a conjurer rolling up his or her sleeves to prove there is nothing concealed there before beginning his act.

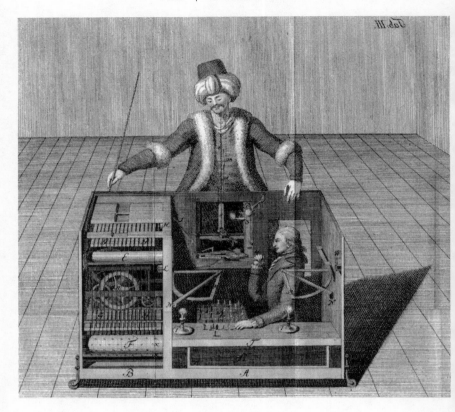

The two doors through which the dwarf entered were concealed by the Turk's robe.

Oh my! Could one think of a better hiding place than the robe of a sorcerer, an oriental one, at that!

Certainly the invitation to the public to scrutinize the apparatus amounts to playing with concealment as a kind of game, which we all enjoy, the audience as much, I guess, as the dwarf and the owner of the apparatus. Everyone is likely to have the sense that the invitation is part of a game, a teasing, a taunting, a game of revelation and concealment. What is more, to equate the dwarf with theology is to recruit not just secrecy but unfathomable mystery. What else is the Messiah, or at least his return?

The ultimate trick is not Rastelli's but a variation thereof related to the return of the Messiah, the most famous instantiation of which is the memorable image in Benjamin's "Theses" of the Angel of History. The angel wishes to return to Paradise but cannot move its wings because the winds of progress blow it into the future while it faces the growing debris of the past.

Could this angel be a metamorphosis of the magical dwarf in the German nursery rhyme flitting through Benjamin's childhood, breaking things, eating his soup, scaring him shitless, watching him but rarely visible except when surfacing at a moment of danger—only to disappear?

16 ART VERSUS ART

In a re-enchanting world in which nature speaks back, the stirring tropes of demystification and enlightenment give way to new possibilities of thought and politics, rhetoric and power—what I will call "art versus art." What sort of art is that, you ask? Well, not to put too fine a point on it, it is certainly not ideology versus truth, nor discourse versus counterdiscourse, but an art of sorcery-speak in a world gone rogue, piling on the negative sacred in which nature speaks through animate impulse and mimetic relays. Whatever the terms, paramount will be the pulse between bodies as America is Made Again.

This amounts to a new human animal aloft with the gift of the bird's wing. What does the bird get in return? was the question we asked at the beginning and what the bird asks of us now, partners in the shamanic trickery of skilled revelation of skilled concealment.

I know noble accents
And lucid, inescapable rhythms;
But I know, too,
That the blackbird is involved
In what I know.

If in 1917 the poet Wallace Stevens could write these lines, how much truer do they seem today?[1]

Art versus art is political activity in theatrical mode motivated by the current dispensation of reality as really made up, joined to the dark surreality of the negative sacred.

Art versus art engages with the art of the spectacle of the twenty-four-hour news cycle, as Fox and the White House indulge their mimetic faculties denouncing fake news about their fake news. How mimetic is *that*, you might ask, the fakers themselves like any old shaman denouncing the others as fakers! Meanwhile the *Washington Post* keeps count. As of April 2019, the president has uttered ten thousand lies since he took office. It is truly hallucinatory, mirrors within mirrors, cycles within cycles, the overarching red cap with its logo in white letters says it all—first the repetition of the return to greatness, the mimetic wheel churning, then the magically mimetic engagement with the fantasy: Make America Great Again. This is art versus art in high gear, which must have been what prompted my friend Professor Todd Ochoa to don a red cap with the slogan Make Mexico Great Again. And let's not forget art versus art when across America countless women donned pussy hats in the first Women's March, which took place the day after the presidential inauguration drew "the largest crowd ever."

Art versus art is companion piece to the metamorphic sublime wherein shape-changing is the order of the day along with camouflage, montage, collage, ventriloquism, and tweetery. The metamorphic sublime is now as prevalent in nature as in the shamanic arts of political theater. In times previous such sublimity was felt and voluble only at times of miracles and emergency, such as the Lisbon earthquake of 1755. In a radio story for kids, quoting eyewitnesses, Benjamin described the earthquake as preceded by purple rain and worms crawling out of the earth. Then the River Tagus was sucked dry by the approaching tidal wave. You can feel the tension as the river is sucked out to sea only to rebound in a massive tidal wave. But today it's purple rain and worms all the time everywhere, and *art versus art* runs where bodies run on automatic pilot outside of language, consciousness, and true or false.

Art versus art is nicely summed up by Antonia Behan writing me that if we study the history of the word "mastery," "to make masteries" includes the performance of a wonderful feat or trick.[2]

There you have it. The compacted, tightly interwoven effulgence of mastery and trickery. Puts you on your toes. Next step, mastery of non-mastery, a trick on top of a trick, a wonder atop wonders—as in artisanal crafts that engage the inner life of materials, with the maker, as we see in profuse detail in Malinowski's descriptions of Trobriand magicians whispering spells into things, spells bound to the poetry of prehistory.

A particular wave I wish to follow here is the rise and fall of the bodily unconscious into and out of consciousness and language, and a good way of doing this is to study a text, as with four examples I have selected almost at random from Marcel Proust's *Swann's Way*, the first of the six volumes of *In Search of Lost Time*.

Here's what I want you, the reader, to be looking for and thinking about:

First, the bringing into consciousness of sensuous detail we don't normally realize we are sensing. As soon as the sensuous is evoked— a smell, for instance, a color, a light-effect—we nod with familiarity, but only because Proust has brought it to our attention and done so either in lavish detail or from a strange perspective, or both. It is only when thus pointed out that the obvious becomes obvious and at the same time acquires other properties because of lattice-like associations specific to context. We could also note that once Proust starts to describe, once reality is worded, the words create other words and worlds without end.

This is the same as what Benjamin alerts us to with what he calls "the optical unconscious" provided by the camera, which brings out visual features of things of which we were unaware, as if we were blessed with a third, magical, eye. The "unconscious" revealed here is not so much inside the viewer as outside-and-inside, bringing to light viewpoints and details of, for example, Karl Blossffeldt's close-ups of a fern, or the way light and shade bring out character in a human face.

In other words, the optical unconscious brings aspects of the bodily unconscious to consciousness. This suggests that Proust's technique of verbal description is the same as or analogous to this occult power of photography—a medium Proust despised because it was, in his reckoning, tied not to involuntary but to conscious memory. Yet with the idea of the optical unconscious it's as if Benjamin met him halfway, pushing Proust into the optical unconscious of photography.

Certainly a still photograph of a person's face, for instance, can bring out optically unconscious, "hidden" aspects of that face and of the person (and this phrase, "bring out" is all-important). Simply holding an aspect of the world still and enframed in a photograph changes it and brings out details we were too busy or habituated to perceive.

What's more, Proust deals with all of the senses, not just the visual, and in fact favors non-optical modalities such as smell, taste, and color as polymorphic magical substance and something elusive we can call "atmosphere," which is a medley of confluent sensations and associations, such as the feel of the sky and the clouds moving across the sky, especially at sunset. Global meltdown, in my opinion, acts this same way, making for a new type of optical unconscious whereby nature is sensed as never before.

The senses are now being reeducated. Meltdown and what I nominate here as Proust's technique of sensory exposition run parallel. Try to imagine his book written today, a century later. Try to imagine the *memoire involontaire* as temperatures hover at 105 degrees Fahrenheit days on end or when hail pours forth midsummer.

Second, there is a lingering in the sensuous as a filigree of connections is displayed, caressed, and turned over; a lingering both sensuous and ideational introducing nonsensuous, even metaphysical, elements and chains of associations. The sensory impression stimulates speculation as well, which is to say sensuousness turning in on itself and examining its grounds. If the young Marx and Engels opined that the senses would become their own theoreticians with communism, then Proust, hardly a communist, has the senses auto-theorizing at full throttle in what we could call a proto-meltdown mode.

The filigree will be at pains to connect outside with inside, the thing observed with the interior of the body of the observer, and there will be frequent allusion to music, movement, breath, and wind. Given this, it is hard not to think of shamanism, at least as I delineate it.[3]

Third, then follows the chasm into which all this filigree is disposed of in the name of an inaccessible secret, meaning the bodily unconscious, meaning Nietzsche's zone of "knowing what not to know."

Bear in mind, too, that *In Search of Lost Time* is ostensibly the work of a man of indeterminate age recalling his youth and thus tinted by the translucency of memory's folds. Here, then, a first sequence of quotes from *Swann's Way*:[4]

But though I remained there in front of the hawthorns, breathing in, bringing into the presence of my thoughts, which did not know what to do with it, then losing and finding again their invisible and unchanging smell, absorbing myself in the rhythm that tossed their flowers here and there with youthful high spirits and at unexpected intervals like certain intervals in music, they offered me the same charms endlessly and with an inexhaustible profusion, but without letting me study it more deeply, like the melodies you replay a hundred times in succession without descending further into their secrets. (141)

The sense of a secret behind the real—the narrator as an adolescent walking along the Guermantes way feeling he can never become a writer or a poet:

> . . . suddenly a roof, a glimmer of sun on a stone, the smell of the road would stop me because of a particular pleasure they gave me, and also because they seemed to be *concealing*, beyond what I could see, something which they were inviting me to come take and which despite my efforts I could not manage to discover. . . . I would concentrate on recalling the line of the roof, the shade of the stone which, without my being able to understand why, had seemed so full, so ready to open, to yield me the thing for which they themselves were merely a cover. (182–83; emphasis mine)

But then come the steeples of Martinville. Riding in a carriage at sunset the young narrator sees the church's two steeples:

> Soon their lines and their sunlit surfaces split apart, as if they were a sort of bark, a little of what was hidden from me inside them appeared to me, I had thought which had not existed a moment before, which took shape in words in my head, and the pleasure I had just recently experienced at the sight of them was so increased by this that, seized by a sort of drunkenness, I could no longer think of anything else.

"What was hidden behind the steeples of Martinville," he senses, "had to be something analogous to a pretty sentence"—several sentences in fact—which he then writes down, mentioning the setting sun several times, as it is this light combined with the movement of the carriage that animates the steeples and makes them almost dance. The writing of this, getting it right, so to speak, by which he means revealing what was hidden, makes him so happy that "as if I myself were a hen and had just laid an egg, I began to sing at the top of my voice" (184–86).

This egg is the egg laid by the premonitory stages of the *mémoire involontaire* but here has little to do with memory per se and does not proceed to the full-blown *mémoire involontaire* effect. For that reason, like the other examples I offer above, it shows us the underlying mechanism of the book as a whole. And what is that mechanism? It is the shamanic act of skilled revelation of skilled concealment. It is the narrator's other self hidden in the sunset-lit steeples (in the sunset, we could say), alive and tensed with the feeling that what is hidden are two things: first, himself and, second, the feeling that what is concealed in the steeples are words, which he then, as some sort of mimetic conduit, puts down on paper, scribbling in the jolting carriage.

What follows is an intensely oedipal moment in which his joyous singing at the laying of this egg gives way to an all-consuming despair as the thought flashes across his mind that he will soon be home and his mother will more or less deliberately avoid kissing him to sleep. It certainly is complicated. He is sad because he can't spend all night crying in her arms.

What this brings out, I think, as you see in the next quotation, is not only the oedipality of the situation but how that situation combines colors and signs into performing the precariousness of play where the body meets language. Inner worlds and outer worlds converge as the setting sun paints a changing sky. It is cinematic:

The region of sadness I had just entered was as distinct from the region into which I had hurled myself with such joy only a moment before, as in certain skies a band of pink is separated as though by a line from a band of green or black. One sees a bird fly into the pink, it is about to reach the end of it, it is nearly touching the black, then it has entered it. (187)

This bird is the narrator, one supposes, but retains its birdness all the same; and it does this on account of the way birds fly at sunset for reasons that are poorly understood, skywriting through fluctuant streams of color.

It seems incorrect and certainly limiting to think of this only as subjective, as if the bird and the bands of color are symbols of an inner state and its longings. To the contrary, is it not also planetary with astral and diurnal rhythms and perturbations bringing on joy followed by intense despair? The "inner states" are also aerial and cosmic, which is why the bird disappears into bands of color in the sky foregrounded by church steeples, signs of divinity.

Indeed, the setting sun, causing color changes in the sky—and not just color changes but the changing intensity of light moving, sparkling, glowing, kaleidoscopic in the roseate dreaming of the setting sun—seems to be the activator of bird life.

Is not the bird disappearing into blackness the withdrawal from language and consciousness into the bodily unconscious of the world?

Following that flight across and beyond the screen of consciousness that is the darkening sky of sunset, we are left with "tremor," something like memory but more a physical and psychic disturbance, like shock-effects or a ship's wake churning aft to the horizon.

This tremor is the aftereffect of becoming briefly conscious of knowing what not to know.

What I mean here by "knowing what not to know" is becoming conscious, as in a flash, of what are normally unconscious bodily processes interacting with other bodies' bodily processes. And by *bodies* I mean my body, your body, and the body of the world, micro and cosmic in one, referencing the human body but also animals, objects, and planetary beings. (Such use of "bodies" perforce includes spirits.)[5]

"Tremor-writing" is of a piece with MNM and both are referenced by Proust's *memoire involontaire* as not just memory but memory that draws upon and enacts corporeal tumult. In the first occurrence of this in his novel, such tumult is cinematic and orgasmic. The suddenly awakened memory, initiated by the taste of the madeleine, opens onto an ever-expanding scene of his aunt, her bed, the quilt, the window opening onto the village of Combray, the fields beyond . . . It seems unstoppable. It seems like it could encompass the world, and what is more, the body of the person remembering is profoundly enmeshed in this unfolding world but, like a lightning rod, shudders in overflowing joy. It is this that lies behind Benjamin's theses on the philosophy of history, with its mix of Marx, anarchism, and the Kabbalah.

Tremor-writing is "after-effect writing," which now includes the after-effect of meltdown, creating the pathway into the mastery of non-mastery for which Proust's book clears the ground. There are two famous paths for walking in Proust, the Méséglise Way and the Guermantes Way. Now we can add a third, "the Meltdown Way."

What is more, the involuntary memorization that is the tremor is not only at work in the body of the observer and is not only subjective but takes place also in what we might call the unconscious of the body of the world, as when Proust notes that a writer sees differently to nonwriters; that the writer has a mental sketchbook that takes in certain physiognomic subtleties that generally pass other people by, such as "puerile trivialities, the tone of voice in which a certain remark has been made, of the facial expression and movement of the shoulders."[6] The greatest artists, writes Proust, "are those who have the power, ceasing suddenly to be themselves, to transform their personality into a sort of mirror—a mirror that transfigures and makes immortal everything that would otherwise vanish."[7]

Could a mimetic theory of art be more clearly expressed?

Yet is the cart here before the horse? Surely it is not that the writer sees better or differently. Rather it is *when one writes* that these "puerile trivialities" are drawn out pretty much effortlessly and unconsciously from their hiding places in the fabric of being.

Such "puerile trivialities," below the radar of the nonwriter, are actually anything but trivial or puerile. They embrace fundamentals, social and physical, and do so all the more powerfully for being below the radar. As has often been pointed out, writing is strange in the way it takes over the writing, takes over the writer's hand and the writer's being. "Death of the author," says Barthes, evoking shamanism and similar states of being during which a person is possessed by a larger-than-life force guiding the song or the hand.[8] Truly a marvel. And the same applies to the reader or, in the case of song, to the listener.

While homage is paid to Proust's concept of the *mémoire involontaire*, it should be pointed out that this event occurs only twelve to fourteen times in the novel as a whole. (This discrepancy itself indicates the blurred edges of the concept or its manifestation.) In other words, most of the three thousand-odd pages are dedicated to near misses—heavily wrought descriptions of sensings, as with the hawthorn hedge, sunset on the Vivonne, and so forth. The work as a whole is far more about what it is to sense, to become aware of sensing, and then let go, leaving an enigma identical to that existing in Freud's model in *Beyond the Pleasure Principle* in which what is brought to consciousness is processed and disappears from memory precisely because it has been made conscious, a curious if not counterfactual phenomenon that parallels, as I see it, the "death drive" (announced in that same book), in which the person collapses into a bodily unconscious state, mimetically at one with the environment.[9] This state is imitated by what is called "playing possum," itself an imitation of death.

Proust insists that no amount of conscious effort at recall will satisfy the nagging sense of a hidden memory stimulated by a sensation.

Only a chance event working unconsciously will bring that to light. (Benjamin pointedly adds that it is not chance at all but the changed character of society and the annihilation of ritual, which alters our modes of perception and remembrance.)

Presumably what Proust regards as the bodily unconscious subtleties of the world that sink into the bodily unconscious that is the mirror of the perceiver, by-passing consciousness, hover in some special zone of access that the art and act of writing sensitizes and sets free. This is why we love and why we hate writing. And why *In Search of Lost Time* is the story of becoming a writer.

Only when he has become what he considers to be a serious writer can the narrator look back and describe that long journey as an odyssey through successive sensory events. It is the *mémoire involontaire* that eventually provides the struggling writer with his theory of writing as arousal of the bodily unconscious. Like Benjamin's flash of the image at times of crisis connecting two disparate points of time only to disappear, Proust's *mémoire involontaire* makes conscious "for a moment brief as a flash of lightning" what is normally never apprehended.[10] As such, the *mémoire involontaire* is separated by Proust repeatedly from the intellect, consciousness, and voluntary memory.

In Proust's words, the *mémoire involontaire* is an *awakening*.[11] It instructs a theory of art in which the cunning of art engages with the cunning of habit (art versus art), understanding habit as itself an art of everyday life based on an infinitude of mimetic practices. Proust's writing is an effort to lovingly prize apart these mimeses so as to better engage with them through what we could call mimetic exercises, raiding not just the bodily unconscious but the memories on which these mimeses are based.

And that is how Proust's novel can teach us to master the arts of non-mastery. For does not the visceral upheaval that is the *mémoire involontaire* come on the back of countless Proustian "near misses" (flashes) that we experience all the time? And does not global melt-down add to these near misses most mightily, grafting our bodies to the ever more misshapen body of the world, all of which raises the question as to whether symbols self-destruct? Can they metamorphose into matter? Is that how they and mastery of non-mastery work?

When I read Proust I become aware that symbols, like plants or any growing thing, have a career or a life-journey. No sooner do they floresce in their full glory, like flowers in spring, than they metamorphose into material bodiedness, jettisoning the symbolic mechanism of meaning, replacing it with something quite different, which is thingness, actuality, bodiedness (there is no adequate term for this) informed by the logic of knowing what not to know. In another language, transcendence creates its own demise into immanence. Benjamin's contrast between symbol and allegory engages with this self-destruction of the symbol into something material and historical, as does Bataille's brief essay on the language of flowers, which emphasizes their short-lived beauty before withering on the stalk and falling into the soil.

Writing on Giotto's paintings, for instance—paintings that to my mind are radiantly symbolic—Proust is enamored of their symbolic power, which to his mind stems from their being so real. He comes to think that the "startling strangeness" and special beauty of the paintings is due to this power to symbolize, but only because they then "descend" (as I put it) into mundane existence. There is a tremendous aesthetic force at work here, a force that is, as he says, "physiognomical," alerting us to the tide-change into bodiedness.[12]

In sum, we confront an everyday yet largely unconscious approach to the symbol and meaning-making. Mastery of non-mastery is exactly this unmaking of meaning as much as its making through the medium of what I call the self-destructive symbol.

Two examples lie embedded in Proust's discussion of Giotto's symbolism. The first concerns the long-suffering pregnant kitchenservant in his parents' home, whose protruding belly continually attracts his attention because of "the weight pulled on it." The example flows immediately from this belly and concerns what he takes to be the thoughts of the dying about which so much myth and so many symbolic outpourings have been made since the beginning of time. But the thoughts of the dying, he suggests, are like the tribulations of the pregnant servant; they are likely to be immensely prosaic and to focus on a basic human need, to drink, or to breathe more easily. That is the "idea of death."[13] (Tolstoy's horrendous story of the slow death of Ivan Ilyich comes to mind.)

The treasure trove of symbolism bound to birth and death rises up into the heavenly sphere only to plunge into the ordinary, the concrete, and the visceral. Although this dichotomy embraces the symbolic versus the actual, it is more than that because "the actual" is not a signified or a referent but exists in the realm of mundane experience, like the weight of a pregnant belly or the thirst of someone dying. This is not symbolic even though it provides the ground zero of symbolism.

This is why Proust's symbolism enthralls me. The intensity of the symbolic power is due to its baroque density of sensuous impressions that eventually auto-combust back into the body with which it engaged. The word-world is dropped into the body-world of the reader. It is what I call, crudely enough, an up-and-down action, and we do well to appreciate the precariousness involved.

Deleuze and Guattari's example of the huge Japanese wrestlers comes to mind. The wrestlers move so slowly you see no movement. Then out of the blue they spring. "What's happening?" gives way all of a sudden to "What happened?" Then back to so slow you see no movement at all.[14]

The authors are here referring to what they conceive of as an invisible "plane of immanence" that under certain conditions becomes visible (what was immanent, or within, becomes transcendent, and without; the concealed is revealed).

Is this not a fine instance of Proust's "up and down" and my idea of the "tremor" left in consciousness?

The question persists. "What happened?"

If we follow the young Samuel Beckett's idea that the issue of habit lies at the heart of Proust, meaning Proust's concern with the censoring function of habit dimming the senses, then in order to free the senses of such a censor Proust's text has to make conscious what the bodily unconscious has been doing all along. Thus, with senses reborn we feel the pull of a new world beckoning beyond the habitual.

It is crucial that this sensuous rebooting is accomplished not by impressionism but by impressions, precise impressions that come at you like thistles, sense-impressions larded with eccentric and unexpected flights of reasoning and associations. Hence there is not only a reeducation as to the fabric of being but a reeducation by the senses of the senses themselves, most notably as regards their interaction with consciousness, of becoming aware of awareness, and then follows the MNM stroke of "knowing what not to know," allowing the body to resume its unconscious wisdom.

As regards the mastery of non-mastery, the point is that habit is mimetic power and only mimetic power can dislodge it. The all-consuming power of habit (William James's "fly-wheel" of society[15]), exists as mimetically implanted force in the body, which is to say in the socially acquired practices sustaining everyday life that may have been millennia in the making; to wit:

For millennia men dreamed of acquiring absolute mastery over nature of converting the cosmos into one immense hunting-ground. It was to this that the idea of man was geared in a male-dominated society.[16]

It seems unlikely that habits of such magnitude could be overcome by conscious rebuttal alone. In which case take heed of the art versus art mimetic pulse, block after block of American cities aswarm with pink knitted pussy hats, claws clenched the day after Trump's inauguration.

17 SUBTERRANEAN CITIES OF SLEEP

Nature provides ample metaphors, but what about nature itself, the way, like war and revolution, it beats up on you so you are no longer able to separate the metaphoric from the horrific because there is no nature anymore because it's all nature now, just like it's all soul as Hurricane Irene and then Sandy come whistling up the island of Manhattan and Trump's Dorian takes a sharp left into Alabama. The metal shutters on the shop windows rattle shut like in some deadbeat town in the third world sealed at nightfall for fear of marauders, as dogs whimper and spirits of the dead knock at the door.

But what about nature in its unspectacular, everyday ways, such as the passage from day to night and back again, falling asleep and waking up—these thresholds creating a perpetual motion machine of emotions bound to cosmic force?

All along in this theater become book I've held fast to the idea of mastery of non-mastery spanning the arc of the everyday, of the sun crossing the sky to disappear into the magic hour of sunset and then sleep. Even sleep, especially sleep, is a repository of the rhythm and energy flows of wheeling galaxies adrift as planet earth cooks. Microcosm and macrocosm: you in your little bed, the universe spinning through you in the depths of sleep.

Crazy! you say. But then, what do you know of what goes on in sleep? "The scientists can describe it," writes Ursula Le Guin, "yet can't claim to understand it. We know sleep in our body, we recognize it as deeply familiar—but the mind cannot lay hold of it."

Contesting the usual contrast of dreams and sleep, she writes, "Dreams may not offer escape, but sleep does. Indeed, it escapes us. It eludes description, it evades. It's what you don't know you're doing while you do it," and, she concludes, "Sleep is hard to talk about."[1]

This maddeningly obvious yet neglected point lies at the heart of Roland Barthes's last lectures, bundled together in the book *The Neutral*. He delights in the fact that a person sleeping has no consciousness of sleep, which is to say that, since the inception of Homo sapiens and of sleep, nobody the world over has had a clue of what's going on one-third of the day, although that could soon alter. Two bug-eyed journalists once accosted me with the news that Dupont was working day and night (!) to eliminate sleep so as to get workers to work more. Shades of Fritz Lang's *Metropolis*! No wonder Dupont, they said, pulped all copies of their book. No wonder! Strange things happen when it comes to sleep.

The wonder of the story is how it serves to estrange sleep, making you wonder what a world without sleep would be like. Given the acceleration and anxiety that is modern life, it is no wonder people ask if sleep is necessary, nor that today just about everyone has a "sleep disorder" and cruises through life jet-lagged on Ambien in neoliberal insomnias clutching a styrofoam coffee cup.[2]

We have seen Proust painstakingly describe the hawthorn hedge, women's dress, and sunset, but it is sleep where his talents most flourish, as when he suggests that sleep is like a second dwelling. It has sounds of its own, servants, and special visitors, and the "race that inhabits it, like that of our first ancestors, is androgynous. A man in it appears later in the form of a woman. Things in it show a tendency to turn into men, and friends into enemies."[3] He expresses surprise that when we wake up we resume the being of the same person we were before we went to sleep. Truly sleep is the great unknown, where all manner of surprises and surmises beckon. Imagine falling asleep wondering if you will wake up the same person, let alone the same gender! The androgyny Proust evokes suggests that when we sleep we become wonderfully multiplex, metamorphic buds capable of all manner of transformations, tricks, and instabilities.

Of course this is not quite the revolution Benjamin has in mind when he equates awakening with revolution.[4] He seems to be thinking more of a shape-twisting form of awakening in which time changes course such that the present is experienced as a world awakening from the dream the past had of it—a fine instance of skilled revelation of skilled concealment, you must admit.

We recall Benjamin's idea that "capitalism was a natural phenomenon with which a new dream-filled sleep came over Europe, and through it a reactivation of mythic force." Yet for all the emphasis on dream that this version of the dialectical image entails, it is locked into the materiality of the human body as part of the body of the world, as the following quotation from Convolute K demonstrates:

The situation of consciousness as patterned and checkered by sleep and waking need only be transferred from the individual to the collective. Of course, much that is external to the former is internal to the latter: architecture, fashion—yes, even the weather—are, in the interior of the collective, what the sensoria of organs, the feeling of sickness and health, are inside the individual.[5]

I have yet to come across a Benjamin scholar willing to tackle this.[6] It must have horrified his erstwhile patrons in the Frankfurt School. Marxists would flee, covering their eyes and ears in disbelief, and Benjamin's most thorough biographers, Michael Jennings and Howard Eiland, would cluck-cluck in dismay. Does it not smack too much of the Nietzschean physiology they assumed he had abandoned in his youth and of the surrealism they thought he had set aside in favor of sturdier sociology?

Drawing on a more literal understanding of awakening, Proust avers that there then occurs an evacuation of all memory, albeit momentarily, so we can begin life again with a blank slate. "We awake," he writes, "not knowing who we are, being nobody, newly born ready for anything, the brain emptied of the past which was life until then."

Waking in the middle of the night, he tells us, "I did not even understand in the first moment who I was; I had only, in its original simplicity, the sense of existence as it may quiver in the depths of an animal."

"I crossed centuries of civilization in one second."[7]

Of course, the sleeping body can be poked and prodded and connected to electrodes while the brain is scanned by wide-awake researchers. But the experience of being asleep is surely a whole lot more than what such scans and electroencephalographs depict? This is an unusual state of affairs. A strange quirk in what makes life life.

Or not? The more you think about it, isn't much of life unknowable on purpose so that life can proceed? Hegel's enthusiasm to analyze the development of consciousness and self-consciousness is only half the picture of what the world, human and nonhuman, is about. The other half is the deliberate and profound abnegation of that. We voluntarily put consciousness and self-consciousness to sleep for long stretches of time every night, and for much of the day too, as do the fish inert in the flowing stream, horses sleeping standing up, and the cat, far more asleep than awake most of the day. Subjectivity and objectivity become meaningless notions for at least a third of a human lifetime, amounting, let's say, to twenty years or more. Asleep in the lovely Catskills during the American Revolution, Rip Van Winkle was a light sleeper compared with this.

Like Proust, Barthes and Benjamin scrutinize the edges of sleep, most especially the edges of falling asleep, waking up, and insomnia. First thing to note, clearing the deck, so to speak, is Proust's serenely unabashed axiom that any description of human life must of necessity include sleep.

"One cannot properly describe human life," he writes in a remarkable passage, "unless one bathes it in the sleep into which it plunges night after night and which sweeps around the body as a promontory is encircled by the sea."[8] Sleep is a journey, he writes,

in the organic and now translucent depths of the mysteriously lighted viscera. World of sleep—in which our inner consciousness, subordinated to the disturbances of our organs, accelerates the rhythm of the heart or the respiration, because the same dose of terror, sorrow or remorse acts with a strength magnified a hundredfold if thus injected into our veins: as soon as, to traverse the arteries of the subterranean city, we have embarked upon the dark current of our own blood as upon an inward Lethe meandering sixfold, tall, solemn forms appear to us, approach and glide away, leaving us in tears.[9]

Kyle Bukhari is dancing this. But it is not easy to journey through one's own body. Not while you are awake, that is. Maybe he is sleepwalking, I mean sleepdancing? Is that possible? He glides. He twists like a fish. He curls like a snake. His mask is white with huge black eyes.

It is a fantastic world, this world of sleep as Proust paints it, jolting us out of our habitual ways of thinking about sleep. Proust's sleep-world is a voyaging world no less fantastic than Julio Reyes's phantom boat (which sails through the last chapter of this book) ascending the Timbiqui River on the Pacific coast of Colombia always at night in layers of darkness with the houses on the riverbanks reflected upside down in the inky river thanks to the light of their gasoline lamps.[10]

Proust's exploration of sleep is like the voyage of that boat up the dark river with its upside-down reflections. We are transported to another world that Proust likens to "that other, vaster, more mysterious, more astral system" as he warns against the censoring power of habit, which the moment of awakening eludes, albeit briefly.[11]

How marvelous it is that he makes a novel out of sleep. How marvelous that he makes a mystery out of sleep's mysteries in which his bed becomes no less magical than an alchemist's laboratory converting base metal into gold. He is the writer-philosopher, poet-biologist, whose work rests on the idea that it is the nature of sleep's nature to undo nature and lift the veil on habit itself.

As for rituals, or rather their absence, is it not strange that sleep is entered into without much by way of ritual given the enormity of the change? Perhaps the lullaby was invented to signal that change, with the infant held hostage:

Rock-a-bye baby, in the treetop
When the wind blows, the cradle will rock
When the bough breaks, the cradle will fall
And down will come baby, cradle and all

A lilting but sinister song with that bizarre line, "When the bough breaks, the cradle will fall." Perhaps it is sung not for the child but for the singer, invoking the tragedy of the fall to forestall even worse fates that might be unyoked by the spirits that emerge at twilight, a fine example of apotropaic magic. The beauty of the melody cuddles the cruelty, concealing and revealing it at the same time. Signaled here, it seems to me, is apprehension concerning the unknown that is sleep for people of all ages and not just the child.

A young artist friend, Isabella Mongelli, who grew up in the south of Italy, tells me her grandmother and mother put scissors by her bed when she was little so as to stop "the monk" or "the black man" coming to her bed at night. You can tell they have visited you in your sleep by a strange twisting of your hair when you wake. Horses develop tousled and knotty hair at night too, and this can only be undone with scissors (of which the devil is frightened).

Later she tells me that the monk and the black man, *l'uomo nero*, are not exactly the same thing. The black man is black on account of his being dressed in black with a hat, his face in shadow. "My auntie used to see him sitting in an armchair in the house. A man in that building suffered a tragic death. The priest was called, and the black man disappeared."

"The little monk—*Monaciello*—comes to visit you while you're sleeping and stays between your chest and belly. You feel vulnerable, unable to breathe, lying there between sleep and wakefulness. My grandma said one time to my sister that he can have the form of a cat."

She adds, "I have heard that the spirits of unbaptized babies and children who have died are unclean, *spiriti immondi*, which can also mean homeless and without country. They roam around teasing people. My uncle, who has a long history of *Monaciello* visits, had two brothers dead before he was born. The little monk came to visit him often, not regularly. He can disappear for one year and come back."

More than dreams, what I gather here is something other than subjectivity and modern psychology, a somaticity aligned with spirit worlds because sleep makes porous the boundaries with Other worlds. To sleep is to die, in more than one sense. Certainly Proust's exploration of sleep is no less fantastic than the world of the *spiriti immondi*. Indeed, he himself seems as close as you can get to *spiriti immondi*, spirits without a home or country, always fabricating one or the other.

From the outset it should be made clear that, like Ursula Le Guin, Proust claims he is not equating sleep with dream. Proust's idea of sleep is an adventure in corporeal metamorphosis attached, as in Isabella Mongelli's stories, to the spirits of the dead and their spawn. It was Proust's triumph and contribution to the world of both fiction and biology to explore and theorize sleep, threading the needle of what Barthes calls the aporia of sleep, the stranger who takes over our body as does death, which has long been equated with sleep.[12] But how richer those aporias become when hitched to the mischief of spirits sitting between your chest and your belly.

As for the sleep that runs through Proust's book, in other parts of the world, as in the indigenous Putumayo region of Colombia where I have done much sleeping, 1971–1997, people sleep differently. They rarely sleep alone, not for lack of space but because they like people close by when sleeping—so different to the ideal of what we might call "bourgeois sleep," whether with a partner or solitary—and they wake often and chat in the candlelit darkness. In Santiago and Ambrosia Mutumaboy's two-room house up there on the ridge above the Mocoa River people would reminisce, laugh, drift off, then wake again. And there is a lot of animal life, in the form of fleas and cockroaches, big ones, at that, crawling over you with their hairy little feet. (How would Proust have taken to that?) Dogs whimper. Cattle stomp in the corral. The river sings its songs. Same on the Sierra de Santa Marta in the extreme north of Colombia, sleeping with the Kogi Indians, men in one hut, women in the other with the children all a-tumble like waves in the ocean. In West Africa, Laura Bohannan experienced this same sort of group-sleep in the 1950s among the Tiv in Nigeria, where she notes that people would wake often, chat, and laugh. With wry humor she notes that an eight-hour "good night's sleep," as we say in the West, was anything but common.[13] When the moon was full, people would sit outside their huts and talk.

Could it be that what has come to be called the "possessive individualism" of the West requires the solitary confinement of sleeping, tucked in tight with the door bolted so that one's cherished private property, one's body and one's soul, can refuel—the car in the
garage put to rest, the cell phone recharging?

Proust, asthmatic and homosexual, wrote alone in the stillness of
night in bed in his cork-lined bedroom. He is not only a night writer
but an insomniac one to the extent that we can conclude that insomnia and night-writing were part of his attempt to break away
from the habit of sleep and hence from convention more generally.

Insomnia was involuntary. Writing was not. Writing was his attempt
to commune with the world at large, making his "own Tiv scene,"
shall we say, of people seated outside chatting when the moon was
full. But being neither Tiv nor Putumayo Indian nor southern Italian peasant, Proust wrote immolated in his soundless bedroom, his
writing turning in on itself in ever more elaborate sentences and
syntax, grappling with the reality of intricate sense-impressions
dancing before his eyes.

Obviously we can't say Proust wrote while asleep. But it seems his
writerly practice is as close as you can get to that. The world sleeps
outside his window. Soundlessness prevails like chloroform. The
maddening proximity of sleep, made unobtainable by the demon
of insomnia lurking over his bed, plagues the narrator. You cannot
but wonder if insomnia provides insight into the unknowable realm
of sleep, or peels away the nature of second nature like the skin of
overripe fruit?

He writes through worlds of sleep at one remove. He is our anthropologist of the sleep-world practicing "participant-observation,"
one moment asleep, the next moment tossing and turning. Insomnia is a twilight zone like that of the magic hour itself.

"For a long time I went to bed early" writes Proust. "Sometimes, my candle scarcely out, my eyes would close so quickly that I did not have time to say to myself: 'I'm falling asleep.' And, half an hour later, the thought that it was time to try to sleep would wake me."[14]

These sentences open Proust's novel.

They also open Walter Benjamin's *Arcades Project*: "Just as Proust begins the story of his life with awakening," writes Benjamin, "so must every presentation of history begin with awakening; in fact, it should treat of nothing else."[15] For Benjamin, this amounted to a new method in which what he called "a dialectical image" surfaces as the awakening of the dream the past had of the present, the wildest of all Benjamin's wild ideas. Like the skilled revelation of skilled concealment, this too possesses a trickster-like, figure-eight quality, in this case of the play between past, present, and future.

But as regards Proust, the quotation Benjamin deploys is misapplied. Proust's awakening is far more haphazard, broken up, and prone to skittish backtracking. Its form is like the baroque light and peripatetic soma of magic hour. Its form is that of Putumayo or Tiv sleeping, not the "good night's sleep" of eight undisturbed hours, but the "broken sleep" of other civilizations.

Proust's novel begins not with waking but with falling asleep and waking up a little later with the thought that it's time to fall asleep. (Did I mention figure-eight circuitry?)

First sleep, then awakening—awakening because, in his sleep, the narrator has the thought that it is time to go to sleep. All this stopping and starting, sleeping and awakening because, in one's sleep, one dreams one has fallen asleep; all this reminding oneself not to forget that one did not sleep; all this confusion and backtracking between sleep and waking—all of this is a reminder of the dreadful solitariness that grips the insomniac, expelled from history, circling the globe of eternal despair.(Did I mention sleep as "second nature" undoing itself?)

He looks at his watch. Nearly midnight. Asleep in a strange hotel, the sleepless traveler is cheered by a ray of light under the door, thinking it is the dawn, only to realize when the light disappears that it is actually midnight and a whole ghastly night lies ahead. Half asleep, half awake, his body serves as a memory-device according to the disposition of his limbs. "Its memory, the memory of its ribs, its knees, its shoulders, offered in succession several of the rooms where it had slept, while around it the invisible walls, changing place according to the shape of the imagined room, spun through the shadows."[16]

Pages and pages of hallucinatory insomniacal prose follow, only they are not hallucinatory at all but the body extending like protoplasmic effluvium into the nether reaches of being. "Everything revolved around me in the darkness, things, countries, years."[17]

Compare that with the night-writing of the American Proust, James Agee, bound to writing as something more like music and cinema. "Night was his time," his companion on assignment, the photographer Walker Evans, wrote, concerning their classic work *Let Us Now Praise Famous Men*, a book in which sleep awakens new worlds, like Proust, waging war on habit.[18]

New biorhythms find their way into prose. At once political ("you have nothing to lose but your chains"), rhapsodic, story-laden, garrulous, and radically mimetic no less than fantastical, it is a modernist text *avant la lettre*, loose-limbed and long-gaited in that American way. It could be an ethnographer's fieldwork notebook.

I want to say that *Agee's words settle like a blanket over sleeping Alabama*. But then I realize that's only half the story. Yes, there is the descent, the sinking and settling of the house and its inhabitants.

A person groans in their sleep. Agee's pencil moves across the page writing in a kid's schoolbook.

Night was his time. In Alabama he worked I don't know how late. Some parts of *Let Us Now Praise Famous Men* read as though they were written on the spot at night. Later, in a small house in French-town, New Jersey, the work, I think, was largely night-written. Literally the result shows this; some sections read best at night, far in the night.[19]

But then comes the ascent into the world of the night creatures, starting with the fish "halted on the middle and serene of blind sea water sleeping lidless lensed." It seems that along with our writer the grammar is a night creature too. The writer seems far from alone.

Agee emphasized that this book was "an exercise in human actuality." If he'd had a second shot, he would have liked it to be photographs along with bits of cloth, cotton, earth, bits of speech, smells, plates of food, and excrement.

Sound familiar? A too-pungent mimesis like that of Saint Anthony alone in his cave in the desert of Egypt two thousand years back?

Must be. Think of them fish "halted on the middle and serene of blind sea water sleeping lidless lensed," and then study Hieronymus Bosch's "lidless lensed" creatures of the deep.

This wish for a collage of things in place of words is a heartfelt mimesis sounding awfully like what Frazer called "contagious magic" in which things talk to things. Agee's prolixity is that of the mad saint desperate to become Other, then Another Other, and so forth on and on . . . desperate to get it all down and right, right there in front of you, as if language is not a tool of representation but a way of being what the writing is about. For getting it all down and right in this case meant a terrifically special form of mimesis concerning the lives being documented, the lives of the sharecroppers, while including himself as an awkward do-gooder and artistic not-rich Harvard boy who loathed beyond measure those labels and most especially the way liberals and the art world would turn his work into a thing to frame and, in a politically very correct way, admire, rather than seek out new ways of being—like his very prose.

"He must not have slept," said Walker Evans.

His gestures were one of the memorable things about him. He seemed to model, fight, and stroke his phrases as he talked. The talk, in the end, was his great distinguishing feature. He talked his prose, Agee prose. . . . It rolled just as it reads, but he made it sound natural—something just there in the air like any other part of the world. How he did this no one knows.[20]

As for the blacks whom Agee barely mentions, he wished at one point he was dead, their faces "utterly without trust of me . . . because in that country no negro safely walks away from a white man."[21]

That alone would make you want to say it different, to develop a new language apt for the American holocaust that was slavery and its continuing Jim Crow aftermath. It is as if the night air of silence, sensory overload, and hallucinatory zoomorphic visions was due not so much to racial segregation as to its unmentionability. The mimetic empathy with the white sharecroppers was the overdetermined cathartic consequence.

Arpeggios ripple like waves in the sea from Anni Rossi at the piano. This is the signature music of mastery of non-mastery.

She sings:

Bone and bone, blood and blood, life and life disjointed and abandoned they lay graven in so final depth, that dreams attend them

seemed not plausible . . . waterhole where gather the weak wild beasts; night; night, sleep; sleep.[22]

Kyle is dancing masked by the waterhole, his eyes glowing:

In the waterhole at night
The body surfaces
Only to subside

Feride Eralp, just the voice:

The dead oak and pine, the ground, the dew, the air, the whole realm of what our bodies lay in and our minds in silence wandered, walked in, swam in, watched upon, was delicately fragrant as paradise, and like all that is best, was loose, light, casual, totally actual . . .[23]

Narrator

Only at the end
Only at the end does the writer fall asleep and the night-writing
   cease

One note on Anni's piano

18 MAGIC HOUR

Falling between night and day, magic hour can be thought of as a performance, one that delights in undoing itself, highly skilled, at that. Of course magic hour is a mode of perception as much as a thing in itself. And of course it is a philosophy realizing the unreality of reality, like taking hallucinogens twice every twenty-four hours, only we don't quite see it that way. But think of Kyle with the white mask and the big eyes dancing through the audience sideways, pivoting—all eyes he is, then all back, then all nothing as the clear notes of the piano light a path with translucent images shining through falling snow, which for this precious moment, act like Agee's waterhole at night doing the Proust thing up and down.

In the waterhole at night
The body surfaces
Only to subside

This is the Waterhole Dance we could call the Mimetic Dance or the Skilled Revelation of Skilled Concealment Dance. And those eyes, great black holes they be, mastery of non-mastery for sure, magic hour for sure, at least as sure as you can be about such things because, enlarging with meltdown so as to colonize more and more of our day, magic hour is signature and motif of mastery of non-mastery.

The light changes, twisting in ever darker blues and spreading shadows such that you get the sensation of bodies moving in a world ever more baroque, which is where as many times as head-on confrontation is called for, so is the indirection of that mastery of nonmastery which Brecht, borrowing from the Tao, described as

. . . that yielding water in motion
Gets the better in the end of granite and
porphyry.

This is certainly germane, this easy flux between nature and culture provided by the poet. By which I mean the way the metaphors move like yielding water themselves between nature and politics, submission and resistance.

Yet are they metaphors? Is not the point with the re-enchantment of nature that the basis of human culture is changing such that we can no longer easily put language and the speaking subject on one side, mute nature on the other?

The dead oak and pine, the ground, the dew, the air, the whole realm
of what our bodies lay in and our minds in silence wandered, walked
in, swam in, watched upon, was delicately fragrant as paradise, and
like all that is best, was loose, light, casual, totally actual . . .[1]

"Totally actual." There is the content (dead oak and pine etc.), but there is also the straining here of language, like the dance undoing itself, straining to become nature and vice versa, in a word, mimetic.

With meltdown the language of nature swamps the nature of language. Benjamin postulated an aspect of this in his remarks on the possibilities for language and image under fascism in relation to surrealism. He was thinking of what he took to be a surrealist-inspired practice setting aside metaphor in place of the body. Crucially this was something more than body, much more, yet intimate with it, what he thought of as a composite, collective *body-image space* galvanized by political crisis.

This body-image space bore a family resemblance to the cinematic body he sketched out at roughly the same time in "One-Way Street," in the section "This Space for Rent," and it appears later too in his essay "Art in the Age of Mechanical Reproduction," wherein the body of the audience is understood to be imploded by the images projected onto the movie-house screen.[2] There is also a resemblance to his notion of children disappearing into colored illustrations, as described in his early essays on color and images in kids' books.

Aby Warburg's idea that images innervate the body of the viewer comes to mind here, especially because of his understanding that a still image is actually a moving image temporarily stilled like a single frame in a movie.[3] Incorporated into my body, the stayed image is then remobilized, as it were, and granted new life, like the one it had before the artist immobilized it.

The emphasis here is on the body as an eye attuned to archives of images gathered through the ages implicating, in the case of magic hour, a fluid merging of the body of the viewer with fluctuant circumambience. If throughout this book I have used "body" as shorthand for my body, your body, and the body of the world, then it is magic hour that highlights this like nothing else, as the eye and consciousness like the sun at sunset disappear over the horizon, leaving in darkening hues a quite other variety of consciousness and a quite other variety of body, while at dawn the process is reversed.

And cannot language, storytelling, for example, enter the body as does cinema to hold me hostage? Of course, it is no longer a "me" but something else for which there seem few words if any, a "me" as ductile presence or intimation thereof, meaning the flow in and out of the worlds conveyed by the language-become-cinema become-image. Thus what in a pre-meltdown era might have been thought of as opposite sorts of things, image and corporeality, are now conjoined in strange ways.

All of which recalls the very beginning of what became first "Sun Theater" and then this MNM book. "We started on a beach facing the Pacific Ocean," I wrote. "The speakers stood. The audience stood. The waves crashed. Language became something else."

That was in 2008, speechifying in nature, anticipating its re-enchantment, forming hieroglyphs in the salt-heavy air.

And something more. What in Benjamin's surrealism essay is called "pessimism," as traced through Dostoyevsky and the patron saint of surrealism, the Comte de Lautréamont (a must read), in which pessimism meant not so much despair as a poetics of the macabre, as tough and iconoclastically relevant to our age of meltdown as it was to the age of surrealism at the time of impending fascism.

To my mind this raises the question of whether the body-image sphere is not universal but historically contingent on just such "pessimism," which I equate with the dark surrealism and metamorphic sublimity of meltdown.

History moves on. The body changes with it. As do the images and image-stock. And yet here we are again, surrealism redux, body-image redux, and the body is for sure a collective body, what the missionary/anthropologist Maurice Leenhardt, based on his twenty-four years with indigenous people in New Caledonia from 1902 to 1926, called *cosmomorphism*, which James Clifford describes as follows:

In cosmomorphic experience the substances of nature actually live in the person. There is no clear separation between self and the world; the same flux of life circulates in the person, in the sap of a plant, in the color of a stone.[4]

He goes on to write that "the experience of identity supposes the collapse of symbolic, even metaphoric relations."

There is no felt distance between subject and object, no mediation of similarity in difference. Cosmomorphic experience is the opposite of anthropomorphism, for a person does not project human attributes onto "nature" but grasps his or her own being as a series of natural events identical to organic rhythms and substances.[5]

This is prefigured for me in the shaping of experience performed by magic hour, its creeping coloration and hollowing out like vapor trails following the glide path of the dancer, each note on the piano punctuating reality into discord vibrant with anticipation.

We could think of the cosmomorphism of magic hour as cinematic, taking note of the change wrought by meltdown. Just as cinema connected our bodies through images with the wider world, so death of the planet reimages the relationships between our bodies and the cosmos. What cinema was to the twentieth century, planetary meltdown is to ours. We move into the future yet backward in time to when mankind was ritually bound to the sky that entered the body.

Follow the dancer.

What used to be but a brief interlude in a diurnal rhythm, the magic hour of twilight and dawn now expands in stops and starts throughout the day as much as through the brain-stem of being.

Thanks to the wisdom of the body "knowing what not to know," this sense of cosmic connectedness is largely unconscious, set by the autonomic nervous system, which is not so much internal to each of us as it is a tremulous node in a vast network of mimetically resonating bodies, leaving barely a tremor in consciousness, ephemeral and fleeting.

The tremors I have in mind are the same as those described in Roland Barthes's last lecture course, *The Neutral*—that ethic, that guide to life lived through twinklings of tact in an anecdotal discourse recruited to outsmart mastery.[6]

The neutral applies with special force to awakening and to falling asleep. Barthes's speculations, no less than his unsurpassingly surprising language, match the moods and light of magic hour. It is as if everything visual about magic hour that catches the cinematographer's eye is here with Barthes expanded into other sensory registers.

Falling asleep and awakening provide an airlock of suspension, "pure moments of Carelessness," he writes, "forgetfulness of evil, vice in its purest state, kind of clear joy in C major; then the earlier Care falls upon you like a great black bird: the day begins."[7]

While sleep presents an aporia, meaning our lack of consciousness of sleep when asleep, awakening on the other hand presents a "hyperconsciousness" involving the visions a person has while awakening, which Barthes understands as a "slack time (between the tides of worry and of excitement), where I see (I sip) life, aliveness in its purity, which is to say outside the will to live."[8]

If Barthes writes of waking and falling asleep as zones of "slack time," Benjamin seizes on such times as weighted with the curious powers of thresholds, all the more curious in his estimate (written in Paris in the 1930s) because "we have grown very poor in experiences. Falling asleep is perhaps the only such experience that remains to us. (But together with this there is also waking up.)"[9]

A radical statement, to be sure. Yet although Benjamin thinks life-crisis rites have largely disappeared, there are a few thresholds that for him still exist at the time of his writing such as the ebb and flow of conversation and the sexual permutations of love-experiences "that surges over the threshold like the changing figures of the dream."[10]

Today, far from disappearing, have not the thresholds of waking and of falling asleep intensified? *Moreover, is not global meltdown itself a momentous threshold?*

We could go further and dwell on the "sexual permutations of love" as threshold phenomena further aroused by the meltdown cosmomorphically coursing through my body, your body, and the body of the world. But that aside, what are we to make of the fact that the threshold that is meltdown suspends us in a continuous becoming, treading water till the inevitable bursts in on us? Will we all die? Will the planet develop strange new forms of life and death such as the giant crocodiles on Florida beaches reported by Fox News or the huge Burmese pythons in the Everglades?

What do you call it when the threshold has become everything and everything is in question, when the in-between is all there is, as with Gilles Deleuze and Felix Guattari's one thousand plateaus by way of Gregory Bateson's take on Balinese culture? How strange. At the end of the world no end. Only middle!

And what of the surreal character of thresholds, especially those thresholds of awakening and falling asleep? Is not surrealism simply a way of envisaging and thinking about thresholds and their magic?

Impressed on the social and individual psyche since the beginning of time, I would suppose, thresholds are key elements of life, collective and individual. Arnold van Gennep brought this to a fine point of understanding in his 1909 essay on rites of passage, but did not venture far into the more philosophical and aesthetic wonders therein, elaborated later by the anthropologist Victor Turner in a landmark essay, "Betwixt and Between."[11]

Focusing on his and Edith Turner's fieldwork in southern Africa, studying an initiation ritual that included, especially for the young men, months-long seclusion from village life, along with special food, dress, and language, Turner makes the point that masks accentuate cultural themes, very much including those of birth and death. Above all there was the taboo of taboo, by which I mean there existed an obligation—not just tolerance but an obligation—to break certain taboos.

But the fuller excitement and beauty of what's at stake is to be found in Benjamin's assertion that surrealism takes advantage of the fact that life seems worth living nowhere but on the threshold between sleeping and waking, across which, back and forth, flood multitudinous images.[12]

Indeed, this could be the leitmotif for MNM itself as much as this book that is not a book but a threshold between a theater and a book. Implicit here is an assumption regarding mimesis: that in this back and forth, image and sound interpenetrate with an "automatic precision and such felicity that no chink was left for the penny-in-the-slot called 'meaning'"[13]

It is as if falling asleep and awakening have taken over reality in our new world of re-enchanted nature, along the lines Balzac noted in the mid-nineteenth century, in which reality and art trade places at twilight:

In the half light the physical tricks used by art to make things seem real disappear completely. If one is looking at a picture, the people represented seem both to speak and to walk; the shadow becomes real shadow, the daylight is real daylight, the flesh is alive, the eyes move, blood flows in the veins and fabrics glisten. . . . At that hour illusion reigns supreme; perhaps it comes with the night? Is not illusion a kind of night for our thoughts, a night we furnish with dreams?[14]

More than illusion is its ambiguity and its uncertainty. As the inimitable Camila Velez writes me, "I've heard Colombian relatives and friends describe the magic hour as the hour in which the dogs cannot be distinguished from the wolves. I looked this up and found it in an article written in *El Mundo*, a Spanish paper which calls it 'la hora del lobo' or 'la hora del lubricán,' which says it is 'the moment when twilight finishes, forms are confused with their shadows, and it becomes impossible to tell if the silhouette that moves in front of the observer's eyes is a wolf or a dog.'"[15]

Camila continues: "The magic hour then is also an hour of transformation, like in the Alexandrian stone the sky has a 'green morning and a bloody evening.'"

Her reference here is to one of the final sections of Benjamin's essay, "The Storyteller."[16] It certainly is appropriate, blending fairytale and sorcery in a rare and prophetic Siberian gem known to myth, referencing not *wolf and dog* but *dawn and twilight*. Petrified in this gem, history as myth is all of a sudden activated, which is pretty much the definition of the dialectical image. It is the sorcerer who can read the signs in this precious moment of a time out of time. And in this case, the future is ominous.

The nearest I know to this Alexandrian stone, in which the sky is a green morning and a bloody evening, is the sky at ten o'clock in the morning turning green and yellow as the hurricane advances on upstate New York. It is magic hour gone wild, cutting the sky mid-morning with an out-of-time twilight and dawn as Lisa unravels her raincoat and slips into it, pulling the hood tight.

This is of a piece with the emergence of the spirits of the dead at dawn and dusk, because the dead, like the sorcerer, are remarkably wolf/dog too, meaning the epitome of trickery, underscoring the fact that it is just such ambiguity with a fair measure of danger that attracts the cinematographer enamored of magic hour, just as it does the storyteller. Yet this is more than ambiguity in that it makes a visceral claim on the body, as does cinema, the claim of spirit possession.

In a flamboyant gesture, trying to come to terms with moving images on the screen, the filmmaker Jean Rouch suggests that in making his films in Niger and Ghana in the 1950s and '60s, both the cinematographer and the camera itself became possessed by spirits, especially when filming rites of spirit possession, as in the making of *Les maîtres fous*.

Outlandish, for sure, yet Rouch's overflowing enthusiasm certainly fits with the considered arguments made by Miriam Hansen in her recounting of the 1930s film theory of Benjamin, Kracauer, and Adorno concerning the bodily impact of cinematic imagery.[17] Now, a century after these film theorists, the movie has changed. It is all around us and inside us and is called, modestly enough, "climate change." There is no sequel planned as yet.

But what sort of bodies am I talking about? Could they be the multiplex chameleon bodies changing shape and sex that Proust discerns while he sleeps, for instance? That would fit with the tumult going on around us today, as if we are now neither awake nor asleep but more like sleepwalkers traveling through our bodies and the body of the world.

The metamorphic sublime of sleep in Proust's account rests on gender plasticity. I am mindful, therefore, not only of the Anthropocene but of the Androgyne as the figure of the mastery of non-mastery that parries and taunts the quintessentially masculine domination of nature and the binaries of gender logic on which such domination is based.

Barthes claims as much in the final lecture of *The Neutral*, and Benjamin does something similar when he picks up on the *imago* of the mother of the storyteller Nicolai Leskov as unable to hurt any living creature and equates her with androgyny, such that "the righteous man" of storytelling is actually "the earthly powerful, maternal male figure," advocate of all created beings and their embodiment as well. Such is righteousness and such is the *imago* of the storyteller, a bisexual environmentalist before these clichés were invented and something more as well, protecting nature not as something "out there" but instead as something that refers us to a cosmomorphic "us" now understood as neither object nor subject, which is surely intimately connected to Benjamin's notion that storytelling abjures explanation.

There is magic and divinity here too, as with the mighty conjuror shamans, male and female, of Siberia, home of the Alexandrian gem, where shamans who could change their sex were likely to be thought of as great healers.[18]

Similarly, in Benjamin's storyteller essay, the bisexuality of a hermaphrodite child "becomes the symbol of God incarnate," forming a bridge between this world and the divine world—that same bridge, I would add, joining twilight to dawn, as in the image sent me by a filmmaker, Marielle Nitolowska, of a view through a window taken at magic hour in Montreal just after the sun had gone down.

It was December and mighty cold there in Montreal. It seemed important that it was an image of a window, not so much of a thing as of an opening onto the world, the world of approaching night complete with street lighting. The entire world was in this frame. The dark pool in the lower half was where we were lost and frightened in the coming-nothingness of existence, while the ice crystals covering the window contained tiny splashes and darts of frosty blue and pink radiating out into particles of nothingness. It was as if the ice crystals by means of their radiant colors had gathered the essence of the entire day so as to petrify existence in the last moments when the sun went down, leaving this fluttering indication that it will return, not as solar dominance but, like the fireflies, as the mastery of non-mastery.

From out of nowhere comes a rippling sound carrying us as chaff on the wind, happy, forlorn, immersing us in time unwinding.

The Dancer dances,
The images filter through the snow
Annie Rossi's music ripples as if forever

While the narrator's seat sits empty.

Was there ever such emptiness?

Yet the music rolls on in crashing waves, which is how this all started long ago on a beach, throwing words into the wind, us standing feet in the sand, heads in a Proustian cloud mass like the icicles colored by the sun below the horizon steady in the night coming.

19 JULIO REYES'S PHANTOM SHIP

These out-of-season ideas began when I was thinking of color and heat by the Timbiqui River in the forests of western Colombia several years ago. I got the feeling that the mimetic faculty, alive in all of nature, including human nature, was picking up on global meltdown, rerouting language and consciousness through the space of death whose shadow, like the setting sun, now claims us.[1]

Poor nature! Melting glaciers. Polar bears adrift in warming seas. Beetles scampering like refugees north and south. Human civilization on the skids, and the poor will go first. Nature the first colony. Nature as victim, an Oxfam basket case with a pot belly and huge eyes staring at you as you evacuate looking for a place to hide.

But hang on. Maybe we should turn this around? Not nature as victim but nature stirring, fighting back ferociously with all it's got by way of animistic impulses and mimetic sympathies, starting with your body as much as with glaciers and polar bears?

It was night. I started to paint a picture of Julio Reyes's phantom boat coming slowly upriver. Just a story, you say, more like a gesture. But how do you paint a spirit ship especially when it's "just a story"? How do you paint a spirit ship at night on a dark river but are unable to paint the different shades of blackness charged with Nietzsche's "knowing what not to know" or, worse still, not knowing what not to know.

Beyond words? Is that why I was painting instead of writing? Or was I searching for a form and a manner of writing that was in itself painting or, better put, cinematic, suited to the delirious circuitry of mastery of non-mastery?

Perhaps the painting, or at least the effort therein, made it real, not really real but sufficiently real in that phantasmatic boat way so that the doors of perception opened wide. Yes! Here it comes tacking through the upside-down reflections of houses illuminated by kerosene lamps glowing in the blackness of the river under a moonless night. Perhaps it was more than I had bargained for. Perhaps it was MNM unwinding the shroud known as "the domination of nature"?

And the waters came, and swept vast numbers
Of creatures through me, so that in my timbers
Creature befriended creature in the gloom[2]

As we drift now like Julio Reyes's phantom boat in our age of meltdown, we sense something new about the idea of being connected and making connections between species as much as between language and species. The ship sinks into a watery grave. Fish, sharks, giant squids, crustaceans of all sorts, and seaweed waving with the currents enter and make a home, temporary as it may be.

But, Whoa! This ship is me! I have become porous to those creatures as much as to the colors of the deep. Friends, we are, now. It seems. We communicate in new ways, now, in the death ship.

But nothing could better represent the shape-shifting formlessness of the mastery of non-mastery than the voodoo light, the time of cosmic gear-change when light and dark slide into, over, and through each other, de-realizing the world, suspending being in becoming.

**It comes as an accomplice, stealthily,
the lovely hour that is the felon's friend[3]**

It is the phantasmagoric light-show called forth with increasing flair
by meltdown, animated by birds, animals, plants, and insects that
awaken as night falls, not to mention those other creatures such as
Proust in bed and James Agee on the porch scribbling with his pencil. Barthes and Benjamin did not think of nonhuman awakenings.
They did not see the bats that suddenly fill the air, lightning fast
they are, gliding in at all angles to consume the mosquitoes that also
love this voodoo light. The fireflies, unlike the bats, exhibit much
calm as they make their entrance as the Nature Theater of Magic
Hour begins.

Fireflies essentially define the word "magic," and as for bats, do
they not come loaded with frightening associations and hence recall Karl Marx, whose words are like bats, said Pareto, being both
birds and mice?[4]

Such a zoomorphic view of language could be taken further when
thinking of the somatic components of magic hour as a multispecies
affair, a dissolution as much as a stalking, preying, and, why not?, a
grand ballet and procession of spectacular forms that slide through,
if they do not actually mimic, the chameleon properties of voodoo
light. We saw this beautifully in Kurosawa's film *Dreams*, where,
hidden behind a tree in the forest, the little boy sees the wedding
march of the foxes dressed like humans as the rain sluices through
the sunlight. "You will die if you see that," his mother warns. But
does he care?

Add to bats and fireflies (and those Japanese foxes) the following
crepuscular beings: ocelots, jaguars, rats, skunks, moose, wallabies,
wombats, nighthawks, owls, and flies, along with a host of beetles
and the deer in upstate New York. And here comes Hegel's owl of
Minerva spreading its wings in flight. A wise bird, for sure, claiming
you only see things for what they are after sunset. Some of these

creatures restrict their awakening to twilight proper, while others extend into the night, especially if there is a moon. And all are exercised by climate change.

Actually, moonlight exerts its own quotient of magic hour independent of the fading sun. Walk outside next full moon, away from streetlights, and feel as much as see reality quaver in disturbing possibilities, including, as Benjamin was quick to point out, your very self quivering as emitter and receiver of mimetic force.

It's not that you see differently. It's that your body "sees" differently at these times of day, even if you don't realize it other than in that "up and down" Proust-inflected way I described earlier—tremors left as the bodily unconscious rises into, then falls away from consciousness, leaving ripples of corporeal excitement like flying fish plowing the wake of history.

Is this what lies in store for us with meltdown, this curious rippling like shamanic trickery revealing only to conceal, not so much beyond language as amplifying its fire-flying potential? Far from being a pathology consequent to meltdown, is this actually a device meltdown provides for a breakthrough into other forms of language and awareness?

"The problem of consciousness," wrote Nietzsche in *The Gay Science*, "first confronts us when we begin to realize how much we can do without it. . . . All of life would be possible without, as it were, seeing oneself in the mirror."[5] The thinking that becomes conscious, he avers, "is only the smallest part of it, let's say the shallowest, worst part—for only that conscious thinking takes place in words."[6]

It is all well and good to be sensitive to the difficulties, yet also the delights, with language (as Nietzsche so obviously experiences and practices throughout his work), but this harsh condemnation seems willfully obtuse, an inspired last gasp of language in its death throes hating on itself, lovingly.

It is all well and good to resort to such anodyne phraseology as "embodied thought," as so many writers on the topic do, but what Nietzsche expresses (I was going to say "has in mind") is not "thought" but something else, which I dare to say is closely tied to a movement of thought rather than thought itself.

It is a movement that cancels itself out in a peculiar and fascinating manner, emerging from and disappearing back into the body, as when we talk of knowing what not to know, or as with conjuring magic based on the skilled revelation of skilled concealment. On this score, language is the ultimate magical trick, nowhere more so than with meltdown forcing us to write without words or, should I say, with words that act like those evanescent spells murmured into things to activate their glow, their speed, their love.

We can agree with Nietzsche about language only if we recognize that there are many sorts of language, of writing and talking and singing and humming, whispering too, in which words engage with my body, your body, and the body of the world in waves of mimetic impulsion, with the dead and the yet to come, not to mention that peculiar property of "voice" skating through the heat and the color you may discern in diary-writing:

Fires had been kindled in a few places. Marvelous spectacle. Red, sometimes purple flames had crawled up the hillside in narrow ribbons; through the dark blue or sapphire smoke the hillside changes color like black opal under the glint of its polished surface. From the hillside in front of us the fire went on down into the valley, eating at the tall strong grasses. Roaring like a hurricane of light and heat, it came straight toward us, the wind behind it whipping half-burned bits into the air. Birds and crickets fly past in clouds. I walked right into the flames. Marvelous—some completely mad catastrophe rushing straight on at me with furious speed.[7]

Walking into fire. Yes! That's us, for sure. This is how I envisage us today, us firewalkers limping behind our fireflies faced with the re-enchantment of the sun in the age of meltdown, roaring like a hurricane of light and heat with birds and crickets flying past frantic in clouds flecked with color in the turbulent slipstream.

And the fieldwork? What if this blur of bodies in flight becomes, along with heat and color, our ethnographic focus? What if the fieldworker practicing participant-observation participates with the birds and the crickets flying past in colored clouds, as can happen when, in *terra incognita*, you write in your fieldwork diary opening up that other fire called yourself?

This is what happens when you take seriously all that magic the islanders have told you about—soft murmurings of spells into things:

like canoe lashings to go safer and faster
fragrant herbs to make love magic
crushed betel nut mixed with pigment to make an intense red
into one's skin to make it glow

What happens if the fieldworker participates in this magic too, whispering prehistory into things as poetry in the present when the subfreezing temperature shot up yesterday to early spring warmth. The snow started to melt like a blowtorch was put to it, and the mist rose from the river like a shroud enveloping all that lay around. We walked in the mountain close to sunset with the streams running high, stripping off our clothes. At times we spooked ourselves, disappearing into the mist like the phantoms we were, same as happens in certain sunsets when the light turns everything purple with shots of yellow and blue raining like vapor from the far-off ridge where the sun sets. The craziest thing was that every few minutes we would walk through a pocket of hot air and then a minute later walk through chill. And the craziest thing was that, as with immersion in the mist, you sensed this mimetic pull into rampant Otherness in a torrent of imminent destruction. Tornadoes were reported further south.

Yesterday, one of those days of utter perfection early fall, it seemed like we were living in glass, the world not real but a picture in which we held our breath.

The End

ACKNOWLEDGMENTS

What an enormous pleasure it was to work with my Sun Theater partners: Anni Rossi on piano and viola; Kyle Bukhari, the dancer; Olivia Taussig, for her animation of the oh! so slowly setting sun colors as permanent backdrop; Bentley Meeker and his crew, for lighting in the Whitney production as well as many suggestions for what, after all, is a theater addressing the political ecology of light in this time of global meltdown; Feride Eralp of the mysterious, anonymous voice; Kira Manso Brown, producer; and Peter Johnson, anthropology PhD student and video maker supreme. In Helsinki I owe special thanks to Harri Lasko of Aalto University for organizing the presentation in a narrow black box theater with a wonderful flautist trained in the Finnish army, whose name I have forgotten. Artist Nancy Goldring suggested the images at the Whitney performance be projected from *outside* the windows, at which point the snow fell.

Artist Amy Franceschini of Futurefarmers created a color scheme for the book's pages so they performed the magic hour of sunrise and sunset, converting the book into a meteorological phenomenon. Such a pity that it turned out to be too expensive. She also performed some of the book in Mexico City and has been its strongest advocate over the many years it has taken to finish.

Simryn Gill's photograph of herself, *Becoming Palm* (which appears as frontispiece in my *Palma Africana*), has been a mainstay for my conception of the "metamorphic sublime."

Filmmaker Marielle Nitolawska not only alerted me to the light of dawn and dusk ("magic hour") but provided the photograph that I describe toward the end of the book, shaping the book no less than does the Sun Theater.

Photographer Dan Torop sent me his photograph of the fireflies in Pennsylvania that anchors my discussion of these erratic wanderers so essential to this work. Diana Policarpo more or less inadvertently buttressed Walter Benjamin's riff on the planetarium in his "One-Way Street" with her and Marie Kolbaeck Iversen's performance of the fall equinox. Kostas Gounis in Crete reminded me of Captain Ahab's Bataillian ecstasy with lightning. Performance artist Isabella Mongelli's stories from her home in Taranto, southern Italy, helped me navigate the aporia of sleep that Proust, Barthes, and Ursula Le Guin made much of.

Decades ago Sayo Ferro of Bogotá introduced me to the Sierra Nevada de Santa Marta and some of her friends there. She continues to amaze me with her observations and stories (her gentle, piquant, manner, above all), which gave me the courage to expand and to flesh out my wild speculations concerning the birth of the sun and its relation to patriarchy, the subordination of the fireflies, and therewith unexpected twists of animism.

My manifold memories of the late Santiago Mutumbajoy (who features so much in my previous book, *Shamanism, Colonialism and the Wild Man: A Study in Terror and Healing*), are everywhere in these pages, too, especially those dealing with the "metamorphic sublime." Tom the Naturalist, from my Sydney *Children's Hour* listening days, popped up out of nowhere, more a specter now, to assist me in thinking through—expressing, I should say—the re-enchantment of nature, first via my memories of his radio stories and later through my memories of his colored chalk drawings on the classroom black-boards.

Jordan Crandall, performance and media artist as well as professor of visual arts, kicked the whole thing off with his invitation long ago to talk in nature about nature—short, sharp, sweet talks as the clouds tumbled and the sea waited on the setting sun.

At the University of Chicago Press my editor Priya Nelson, together with Dylan Montanari, kept me and things on track in their graceful and inventive ways, while Joel Score, with the patience of Job, performed wonders as copy editor.

Finally, I wish to acknowledge the Andy Warhol Foundation for the Visual Arts for a grant that allowed me a semester off teaching to start on this work.

NOTES

ONE

1 Theodor W. Adorno, "On Walter Benjamin," in *Prisms* (Cambridge, MA: MIT Press, 1986).

2 Adorno, "On Walter Benjamin," 233.

3 Walter Benjamin, "On the Mimetic Faculty" [1933], in *Reflections*, ed. Peter Demetz, 335–36 (New York: Harcourt Brace Jovanovich, 1978).

4 James George Frazer, *The Golden Bough*, part 1, *The Magic Art and the Evolution of Kings*, 3rd ed. (London: Macmillan, 1920), 52 ff.

5 Remark by Steve Feld following a presentation I made on mimesis at the University of Texas at Austin many years ago.

6 Filmmaker and cultural anthropologist Jean-Paul Colleyn, a close friend of Rouch, tells me that the cracked egg was actually Rouch's invention. It was he who broke the egg over the governor's head!

TWO

1 Roland Barthes, *The Neutral: Lecture Course at the Collège de France (1977–1978)*, trans. Rosalind E. Krauss and Denis Hollier (New York: Columbia University Press, 2005), 10–30.

2 Lesley Stern, Alphonso Lingis, and Niklaus Largier were the other "solar speakers."

3 Thomas Pynchon, *Gravity's Rainbow* (New York: Penguin, 1973), 113

4 Roland Barthes, *The Neutral: Lecture Course at the Collège de France (1977–1978)*, trans. Rosalind E. Krauss and Denis Hollier (New York: Columbia University Press, 2005), 10–30.

5 Barthes, *The Neutral*, 10.

THREE

1   Friedrich Nietzsche, introduction to *Twilight of the Idols*, in *Twilight of the Idols and The Anti-Christ; or, How to Philosophize with a Hammer*, ed. Michael Tanner, trans. R. J. Hollingdale (New York: Penguin, 1990), 32. It was Tom (W. J. T.) Mitchell who alerted me to the charm of Nietzsche's tuning fork.

2   Michael Young, *Malinowski: Odyssey of an Anthropologist, 1884-1920* (New Haven, CT: Yale University Press, 2004). See also the audiobook *Taim Bilong Masta*, oral histories assembled by Timothy Bowden with a wealth of detail concerning the culture of the whites in Papua New Guinea.

3   Young, *Malinowski*, 529, 528. On bluff and mimesis see also Sasha Newell, *The Modernity Bluff: Crime, Consumption, and Citizenship in Côte d'Ivoire* (Chicago: University of Chicago Press, 2012).

4   Bertolt Brecht, "The Anxieties of the Regime," in *Bertolt Brecht: Poems, 1913-1956* (1976; New York: Routledge, 1987), 296-98.

5   Max Horkheimer and Theodor Adorno, "Elements of Anti-Semitism," in *Dialectic of Enlightenment* (Stanford, CA: Stanford University Press, 2002), 137-72.

6   Horkheimer and Adorno, *Dialectic of Enlightenment*, 35-62.

7   Franz Kafka, "The Silence of the Sirens," in *Kafka: The Complete Stories*, ed. Nahum N. Glatzer (New York: Schocken, 1971), 430-32.

8   Friedrich Nietzsche, *The Gay Science: With a Prelude in Rhymes and an Appendix of Songs*, ed. Bernard Williams, trans. Josefine Nauckhoff (Cambridge: Cambridge University Press, 2001), §344, 201. I have replaced "polytropoi" with "swindlers."

9   Gustave Flaubert, *The Temptation of St. Anthony*, trans. Kitty Mrosovsky (Harmondsworth: Penguin, 1983).

FOUR

1   Friedrich Nietzsche, *Thus Spoke Zarathustra*, trans. R. J. Hollingdale (London: Penguin, 1961).

FIVE

1   Georges Bataille, *The Accursed Share*, vols. 2-3 (New York: Zone, 1991), 209.

2   Bataille, *Accursed Share*, 14

3   Michel Foucault, "A Preface to Transgression," in *Language, Counter-Memory, Practice*, ed. Donald F Bouchard (Ithaca, NY: Cornell University Press, 1977), 35.

4   Foucault, "Preface to Transgression," 44.

5   Nietzsche, *Gay Science*, §125, 120.

6 Michael Herr, *Dispatches* (New York: Vintage, 1991).

7 John Berger, *The Moment of Cubism and Other Essays* (New York: Pantheon, 1969).

8 Michael Taussig, *Law in a Lawless Land* (Chicago: University of Chicago Press, 2003).

9 James Comey, "How Trump Co-opts Leaders Like Bill Barr," *New York Times*, May 2, 2019.

10 Nietzsche, *The Birth of Tragedy*, second preface, trans. Walter Kauffman (New York: Random House, 1967).

SIX

1 Michael Taussig, *Palma Africana* (Chicago: University of Chicago Press, 2018).

2 For example, Goffman, *Presentation of the Self in Everyday Life* (New York: Doubleday, 1959).

3 Taussig, *Palma Africana*; Juan Felipe Garcia, *El Exterminio de la isla de Papayal* (Bogota: Editorial Pontifica Universidad Javeriana, 2019).

4 *Palma de aceite colombiana* (Bogotá: Villegas Editores, 2013).

5 This photograph appears as the frontispiece to Taussig, *Palma Africana*.

6 *Palma de aceite colombiana*.

7 Taussig, *Palma Africana*, 173.

8 Erland Nordenskiold and Ruben Pérez Kantule, *An Historical and Ethnographic Study of the Cuna Indians*, ed. Henry Wassen (Goteburg: Etnografiskamuseet, 1938).

9 Michael Taussig, *Mimesis and Alterity* (London: Routledge, 1993), 126–28.

10 Roger Caillois, "Mimickry and Legendary Psychaesthenia," *October*, no. 31 (Winter 1984); originally in *Minotaure* 7 (1935).

11 See, for example, David Attenborough on the BBC, "Wild Orchid Wasp Mimic," https://www.youtube.com/watch?v=h813cqpgnA.

SEVEN

1 See Georges Bataille, "The Obelisk," 213–22, in *Visions of Excess: Selected Writings, 1927–1939*, ed. Allan Stoekl, trans. Allan Stoekl with Carl R. Lovitt and Donald M. Leslie Jr. (Minneapolis: University of Minnesota Press, 2002).

2 Walter Benjamin, *The Arcades Project*, ed. Rolf Tiedemann, trans. Howard Eiland and Kevin McLaughlin (Cambridge, MA: Belknap Press, 1999), 102.

3 D. H. Lawrence, *Apocalypse and the Writings on Revelation*, ed. Mara Klanins (Cambridge: Cambridge University Press, 2002), 76–78.

4 Emily Dickinson, "The Last Night That She Lived," in *The Selected Poems of Emily Dickinson* (New York: Modern Library, 1996), 207.

5   Benjamin, "Theses on the Philosophy of History," in *Illuminations*, 254–55.

6   Benjamin, *Arcades Project*, 388.

7   Theodor W. Adorno, "A Portrait of Walter Benjamin," in *Prisms*, trans. Samuel Weber and Shierry Weber (Cambridge, MA: MIT Press, 1981), 240.

EIGHT

1   Ralph Waldo Emerson, "Nature," in *Essays and Lectures* (New York: Library of America, 1983), 9–10.

2   Found by Amy Franceschini on a northern California campus.

3   Benjamin, "One-Way Street," in *Reflections*, 92.

4   Benjamin, "One-Way Street," in *Reflections*, 93.

5   Benjamin, "One-Way Street," in *Reflections*, 93.

6   Benjamin, "One-Way Street," in *Reflections*, 93.

7   Pedro Calderón de la Barca, *Life Is a Dream*, trans. Edward Fitzgerald, http://www.gutenberg.org/ebooks/6363.

NINE

1   Walter B. Cannon, *The Wisdom of the Body* (New York: Norton, 1932).

2   David Foster Wallace, "How Tracy Austin Broke My Heart," in *Consider the Lobster and Other Essays* (New York: Little, Brown and Company, 2005).

3   Philippe Ariès, *Centuries of Childhood: A Social History of Family Life* (New York: Vintage, 1962).

4   Peter Lamborn Wilson, *Utopian Traces* (New York: Logosophia, 2019).

5   George Lucas, *Star Wars* (New York: Ballantine, 1976), facing page 108.

TEN

1   Müller, cited in Richard M. Dorson, "The Eclipse of Solar Mythology," *Journal of American Folklore* 68, no. 270 (1955): 399.

2   Miguel de Cervantes, *Don Quixote de la Mancha*, trans. Peter Motteux (New York: Random House, 1941), 33.

3   The mimetic faculty flourishes with the human body as self-reference. This is brought out in a beguiling note Benjamin wrote in 1936: "The knowledge that the first material on which the mimetic faculty tested itself was the human body should be used more fruitfully than hitherto to throw light on the primal history [*Urgeschichte*] of the arts. . . . Perhaps Stone Age man produced such incomparable drawings of the elk only because the hand guiding the implement remembered the bow with which it had felled the beast." Walter Benjamin, *Gesammelte Schriften*, 6:127. Translation by Edmund Jephcott in Benjamin, *Selected Writings*,

vol. 3, *1935–1938*, ed. Howard Eiland and Michael W. Jennings, trans. Edmund Jephcott, Howard Eiland, et al. (Cambridge, MA: Belknap Press, 2002), 253.

4 Nietzsche, *Genealogy of Morals* (Cambridge: Cambridge University Press, 1994), 61. David Foster Wallace, "How Tracy Austin Broke My Heart," in Consider the Lobster and Other Essays (New York: Back Bay, 2007).

5 Richard Pevear, foreword to Fyodor Dostoevsky, *Crime and Punishment* (New York: Vintage, 1991), x–xi.

6 Foreword, in Fyodor Dostoevsky, *Crime and Punishment*, trans. Richard Pevear and Larissa Volokhonsky (New York: Vintage, 1993), x.

7 Patrick Leigh Fermor, *Mani: Travels in the Southern Peloponnese* [1968] (New York: New York Review Books, 2006), 31.

8 See Nietzsche, *Twilight of the Idols*, IV, 6.

9 James Barron, "Volunteering to Document the Weather, for 84 Years," *New York Times*, August 6, 2014.

10 Barron, "Volunteering."

11 Walter Benjamin, "In the Sun," in *Selected Writings*, vol. 2, *1927–1934*, ed. Michael W. Jennings, Howard Eiland, and Gary Smith, trans. Rodney Livingston et al. (Cambridge, MA: Belknap Press, 1999), 662–65.

12 Vicente Valero, *Experiencia y pobreza: Benjamin en Ibiza, 1932–1933* (Barcelona: Ediciones Peninsula, 2001).

13 Walter Benjamin, "Theses on the Philosophy of History," in *Illuminations: Essays and Reflections*, ed. Hannah Arendt, trans. Harry Zohn (New York: Schocken, 1968), 262–63.

ELEVEN

1 Email from Dan Torop accompanying his photograph of fireflies.

2 Pier Paolo Pasolini, "Il vuoto del potere in Italia," *Corriere della Sera*, February 1, 1975.

3 Fredric Jameson, *Late Marxism: Adorno, or the Persistence of the Dialectic* [1990] (New York: Verso, 2007), 67

4 Pasolini, "Il vuoto del potere in Italia."

5 Georges Didi-Huberman, *Survivance des lucioles* (Paris: Éditions de Minuit, 2009) and *L'image survivante* (Paris: Éditions de Minuit, 2002).

6 Donald Tayler, *The Coming of the Sun, a Prologue to Ika Sacred Narrative*, Pitt Rivers Museum Monograph no. 7 (Oxford: University of Oxford, 1997).

7 Brion Gysin, interviewed by Terry Wilson, in *Here to Go: Planet R-101* (San Francisco: Re/Search Publications, 1982), 240

8 Néstor Almendros, *A Man with a Camera*, trans. Rachel Phillips Belasch (New York: Farrar, Strauss & Giroux, 1984), 182.

9 Nietzsche, *Thus Spoke Zarathustra*, trans R. J. Hollingdale (London: Penguin,

1961), 46; quoted in Howard Caygill, *On Resistance: A Philosophy of Defiance* (London: Bloomsbury, 2013), 170.

10   Thomas Pynchon, *Gravity's Rainbow* [1973] (New York: Penguin, 1995), 336.

11   Michael Taussig, "Darkness at Noon," in Johanna Lundberg, *Finnish Landscape* (Helsinki: Garret, 2016), 165–78.

TWELVE

1   Tayler, *Coming of the Sun*.

2   Gerardo Reichel-Dolmatoff and Alicia Reichel-Dolmatoff, *The People of Aritama: The Cultural Personality of a Colombian Mestizo Village* (London: Routledge, 1961), 349–51.

3   See Michael Taussig, *Defacement: Public Secrecy and the Labor of the Negative* (Stanford, CA: Stanford University Press, 1999), part three, 99–219. See also Anne Chapman, *Hain: Initiation Ceremony of the Selknam of Tierra Del Fuego* (Buenos Aires: Zagier & Urruty, 2008), 39–41.

4   Taussig, *Defacement*.

5   Taussig, *Defacement*, 111. The quotation is from Johannes Wilbert, "The Origin of the Women's Kloketen," in *Folk Literature of the Selknam Indians: Martin Gusinde's Collection of Selknam Narratives* (Los Angeles: UCLA Latin America Center Publications, 1975), 147–61.

6   Nietzsche, *Twilight of the Idols*, 84.

7   Taussig, *Defacement*, 114.

8   Taussig, *Defacement*, 114.

9   Taussig, *Defacement*, 114.

10   Chapman, *Hain*, 39.

11   Alberto Harambour, *Un viaje a las colonias: Memorias y diario de un overjero escoses en Malvinas, Patagonia y Tierra del Fuego (1878–1898)* (Santiago: Dirección de Bibliotecas, Archivos y Museos, 2016).

THIRTEEN

1   Bataille, "The Obelisk."

2   Giambattista Vico, *The New Science of Giambattista Vico* [1725–1744], trans. T. Bergin and M. Fisch (Ithaca, NY: Cornell University Press, 1970), 74 ff.

3   Robert Lebel and Isabelle Waldberg, eds., *Encyclopaedia Acephalica* (London: Atlas Press, 1995), 15.

4   Bataille, "Sacrifice," 121.

5   Annette Michelson, "Heterology and the Critique of Instrumental Reason," *October*, no. 36 (1986): 111.

6   Michel Foucault, *Language, Counter Memory, Practice: Selected Essays and Inter-*

views [1963], ed. Donald F. Bouchard, trans. Donald F. Bouchard and Sherry Simon (Ithaca, NY: Cornell University Press, 1977), 37, 35.

7 Georges Bataille, *The Accursed Share: An Essay on General Economy*, vol. 1, *Consumption*, trans. Robert Hurley (New York: Zone Books, 1988), 21.

8 Herman Melville, *Moby Dick; or, The Whale*, ed. Harrison Hayford, Hershel Parker, and G. Thomas Tanselle (Evanston, IL: Northwestern University Press, 1994), 119–20. Many thanks to Kostas Gounis for directing me to this and subsequent references to lightning in *Moby Dick*.

9 *Moby Dick*, 502.

FOURTEEN

1 *Economic and Philosophic Manuscripts of 1844*, in *The Marx-Engels Reader*, 2nd ed., ed. Robert C. Tucker (Princeton, NJ: Princeton University Press, 1978), 87–88.

2 Bronislaw Malinowski, *Coral Gardens and Their Magic* [1935] (Bloomington: Indiana University Press, 1965), 1:105–6.

3 Malinowski, *Coral Gardens*, 1:129–30.

4 Malinowski, *Coral Gardens*, 1:129.

FIFTEEN

1 Roger Caillois, "Mimicry and Legendary Psychasthenia" [1935], trans. John Shepley, *October*, no. 31 (1984): 16–32.

2 Joseph Berger, "He Told the Story of Bridging the Narrows," *New York Times*, July 2, 2014.

3 Berger, "He Told the Story."

4 Walter Benjamin, "Rastelli's Story," in *Selected Writings*, 3:96–98.

5 Benjamin, "Rastelli's Story," in *Selected Writings*.

6 Benjamin, *Selected Writings*, 2:591, 643.

7 Tom Standage, *The Turk: The Life and Times of the Famous Eighteenth-Century Chess Playing Machine* (New York: Walker, 2002), 22–23.

SIXTEEN

1 Wallace Stevens, "Thirteen Ways of Looking at a Blackbird." See Aaron M. Moe, *Zoopoetics: Animals and the Making of Poetry* (Lanham, MD: Lexington Press, 2014), 6.

2 Antonia Behan, "Craft and the Mastery of Non-Mastery," seminar paper, Department of Anthropology, Columbia University, Fall 2014.

3 Michael Taussig, "Viscerality, Faith, and Skepticism: Another Theory of Magic"

[1998], in *Walter Benjamin's Grave* (Chicago: University of Chicago, 2006). See also Taussig, *Shamanism, Colonialism, and the Wild Man* (Chicago: University of Chicago Press, 1987).

4 Marcel Proust, *In Search of Lost Time*, vol. 1, *Swann's Way*, trans. Lydia Davis (New York: Viking, 2003).

5 See Taussig, *Mimesis and Alterity*, xx; see also Spinoza's use of bodies as, e.g., referenced by Jane Bennett, *Vibrant Matter: A Political Ecology of Things* (Durham, NC: Duke University Press, 2010).

6 Marcel Proust, *Time Regained* (New York: Modern Library, 1993), 306.

7 Proust, *In The Shadow of Young Girls in Flower*, vol. 2 of *In Search of Lost Time*, cited by Benjamin Taylor, *Proust: The Search* (New Haven, CT: Yale University Press, 2015), 167.

8 Roland Barthes, "Death of the Author," in *Image-Music-Text* (New York: Hill and Wang, 1978).

9 See Horkheimer and Adorno on the death drive, as quoted in Taussig, *Mimesis and Alterity*, 46.

10 Proust, *Time Regained*, 264.

11 This is the same as Benjamin's focus on awakening (and sleeping) in his Convolute K, this focus being the basis of the Paris Arcades project.

12 Proust, *Swann's Way*, 83–84.

13 Proust, *Swann's Way*, 110–13.

14 Gilles Deleuze and Felix Guattari, *A Thousand Plateaus* (Minneapolis: University of Minnesota Press, 1987), 281.

15 A flywheel is a heavy wheel affixed to a revolving shaft so as to even out the spasms, bumps, slow-downs, and speed-ups in the rotation. With meltdown, however, the spasms become too great and the flywheel itself starts to spasm and bump.

16 Horkheimer and Adorno, *Dialectic of Enlightenment*, 206.

SEVENTEEN

1 Ursula K. Le Guin, "Great Nature's Second Course," *Words Are My Matter: Writings about Life and Books, 2000–2016* (Easthampton: Small Beer Press, 2016).

2 Michael Taussig, "The Go Slow Party," in *The Corn Wolf* (Chicago: University of Chicago Press, 2015), 138–52.

3 Marcel Proust, *In Search of Lost Time*, vol. 4, *Sodom and Gomorrah*, trans. C. K. Scott Moncrieff and Terence Kilmartin, rev. D. J. Enright (New York: Modern Library, 1993), 516–17.

4 It is strange that despite his translating one volume of Proust, and despite the crucial part played by awakening in *The Arcades Project*, Benjamin did not in his essay on Proust focus on the singular importance of falling sleep.

5   Benjamin, K1, 5, in Convolute K, "Dream City and Dream House . . . ," in *Arcades Project*, 389.

6   But see Miriam Bratu Hansen, *Cinema and Experience: Siegfried Kracauer, Walter Benjamin, and Theodor W. Adorno* (Berkeley: University of California Press, 2011); Eric Santner, *On Creaturely Life: Rilke, Benjamin, Sebald* (Chicago: University of Chicago Press, 2006); Sigrid Weigel, *Body and Image-Space: Re-Reading Walter Benjamin* (London: Routledge, 1996); and Steven Shaviro, *The Cinematic Body* (Minneapolis: University of Minnesota Press, 1993).

7   Proust, *Swann's Way*, 5–6.

8   Marcel Proust, *In Search of Lost Time*, vol. 3, *The Guermantes Way*, trans. C. K. Scott Moncrieff and Terence Kilmartin, rev. D. J. Enright (New York: Modern Library, 1993), 106.

9   Proust, *Sodom and Gomorrah*, 216.

10 See Taussig, *My Cocaine Museum* (Chicago: University of Chicago Press, 2004).

11 Proust, *Sodom and Gomorrah*, 518.

12 Barthes, *The Neutral*, 37–39.

13 Laura Bohannan, *Return to Laughter* [1954] (New York: Natural History Library, 1964).

14 Proust, *Swann's Way*, 3.

15 Benjamin, Convolute N, in *Arcades Project*, 464.

16 Proust, *Swann's Way*, 6.

17 Proust, *Swann's Way*, 6.

18 James Agee and Walker Evans, *Let Us Now Praise Famous Men* [1939] (New York: Houghton Mifflin, 1960).

19 Walker Evans, "Foreword: James Agee in 1936," in *Let Us Now Praise Famous Men*, xi.

20 Evans, "Foreword," xi.

21 Agee and Evans, *Let Us Now Praise*, 42.

22 Agee and Evans, *Let Us Now Praise*, 20.

23 Agee and Evans, *Let Us Now Praise*, 225.

EIGHTEEN

1   Agee and Evans, *Let Us Now Praise*, 225.

2   See Shaviro, *Cinematic Body*; Weigel, *Body and Image-Space*.

3   See Georges Didi-Huberman, *The Surviving Image: Phantoms of Time and Time of Phantoms: Aby Warburg's History of Art*, trans. Harvey Mendelsohn (University Park: Pennsylvania State University Press, 2016).

4   James Clifford, *Person and Myth: Maurice Leenhardt in the Melanesian World* (Berkeley: University of California Press, 1982), 173.

5   Clifford, *Person and Myth*, 174.

6 Barthes, *The Neutral*, 30.

7 Barthes, *The Neutral*, 37.

8 Barthes, *The Neutral*, 38.

9 Benjamin, Convolute O, "Prostitution, Gambling," in *Arcades Project*, 494.

10 Benjamin, Convolute O, in *Arcades Project*.

11 Victor Turner, *In the Forest of Symbols: Aspects of Ndembu Ritual* (Ithaca, NY: Cornell University Press, 1967).

12 Benjamin, "Surrealism: The Last Snapshot of the European Intelligentsia" [1929], in *Reflections*, 182–83.

13 Benjamin, "Surrealism," in *Reflections*.

14 Honoré de Balzac, "The Purse," in *Selected Short Stories*, trans. Sylvia Raphael (New York: Penguin, 1977).

15 Compare with David Levi-Strauss, *Between Dog and Wolf*.

16 Benjamin, "The Storyteller: Reflections on the Work of Nikolai Leskov," [1936], in *Illuminations*, 83–100.

17 Hansen, *Cinema and Experience*.

18 Taussig, "Viscerality, Faith, and Skepticism."

NINETEEN

1 Taussig, *My Cocaine Museum*, esp. the section on heat; see also chapter 3, "Where Stones Walk Like Men," in *What Color Is the Sacred?* (Chicago: University of Chicago Press, 2009).

2 Brecht, "The Ship," in *Bertolt Brecht: Poems, 1913–1956*.

3 Charles Baudelaire, "Twilight: Evening," in *Les Fleurs du Mal*, 99–100, trans. Richard Howard (Boston: David R. Godine, 1982).

4 Bertell Ollman, *Alienation: Marx's Concept of Man in Capitalist Society* (Cambridge: Cambridge University Press, 1971).

5 Nietzsche, *Gay Science*, §354, 211–12.

6 Nietzsche, *Gay Science*, 213

7 Bronislaw Malinowski, *A Diary in the Strict Sense of the Term*, 2nd ed. [1967] (London: Althone, 1989), 11–12.

WORKS CITED

Adorno, Theodor W. *Aesthetic Theory* [1970]. Edited by Gretel Adorno and Rolf Tiedemann. Translated by Robert Hullot-Kentor. New York: Continuum, 2004.

———. "The Idea of Natural History." Translated by Robert Hullot-Kentor. *Telos* 60 (1984): 111–24.

———. "A Portrait of Walter Benjamin." In *Prisms*, 227–41. Translated by Samuel Weber and Shierry Weber. Cambridge, MA: MIT Press, 1981.

Agee, James, and Walker Evans. *Let Us Now Praise Famous Men* [1939]. New York: Houghton Mifflin, 1960.

Almendros, Néstor. *A Man with a Camera.* Translated by Rachel Phillips Belasch. New York: Farrar, Straus & Giroux, 1984.

Ariès, Philippe. *Centuries of Childhood: A Social History of Family Life.* New York: Vintage, 1962.

Balzac, Honoré de. "The Purse." In *Selected Short Stories.* Translated by Sylvia Raphael. New York: Penguin, 1977.

Barron, James. "Volunteering to Document the Weather, for 84 Years." *New York Times*, August 6, 2014.

Barthes, Roland. *The Neutral: Lecture Course at the Collège de France (1977–1978).* Translated by Rosalind E. Krauss and Denis Hollier. New York: Columbia University Press, 2005.

Bataille, Georges. *The Accursed Share: An Essay on General Economy* [1949]. Vol. 1, *Consumption.* Translated by Robert Hurley. New York: Zone Books, 1988.

———. *The Accursed Share: An Essay on General Economy* [1949]. Vols. 2 and 3, *The History of Eroticism* and *Sovereignty.* Translated by Robert Hurley. New York: Zone Books, 1991.

———. "The Obelisk." In *Visions of Excess: Selected Writings, 1927–1939*, 213–22. Edited by Allan Stoekl. Translated by Allan Stoekl with Carl R. Lovitt and Donald M. Leslie Jr. Minneapolis: University of Minnesota Press, 2002.

———. "Sacrifice." *October*, no. 36 (1986): 61–74.

Baudelaire, Charles. "Twilight: Evening." In *Les Fleurs du Mal*, 99–100. Translated by Richard Howard. Boston: David R. Godine, 1982.

Behan, Antonia. "Craft and the Mastery of Non-Mastery." Seminar paper. Department of Anthropology, Columbia University, Fall 2014.

Benjamin, Walter. *The Arcades Project*. Edited by Rolf Tiedemann. Translated by Howard Eiland and Kevin McLaughlin. Cambridge, MA: Belknap Press, 1999.

———. *Illuminations: Essays and Reflections*. Edited by Hannah Arendt. Translated by Harry Zohn. New York: Schocken, 1968. "The Storyteller: Reflections on the Work of Nikolai Leskov" [1936], 83–100. "Theses on the Philosophy of History," 253–64.

———. *Reflections: Essays, Aphorisms, Autobiographical Writings*. Edited by Peter Demetz. Translated by Edmund Jephcott. New York: Harcourt Brace Jovanovich, 1978. "One-Way Street" [1928], 45–106. "On the Mimetic Faculty" [1933], 333–36. "Surrealism: The Last Snapshot of the European Intelligentsia" [1929], 177–92.

———. *Selected Writings*. Vol. 2, *1927–1934*. Edited by Michael W. Jennings, Howard Eiland, and Gary Smith. Translated by Rodney Livingston et al. Cambridge, MA: Belknap Press, 1999. "In the Sun," 662–65.

———. *Selected Writings*. Vol. 3, *1935–1938*. Edited by Howard Eiland and Michael W. Jennings. Translated by Edmund Jephcott, Howard Eiland, et al. Cambridge, MA: Belknap Press, 2002. "Rastelli's Story," 000–00.

Bennett, Jane. *Vibrant Matter: A Political Ecology of Things*. Durham: Duke University Press, 2010.

Berger, Joseph. "He Told the Story of Bridging the Narrows." *New York Times*, July 2, 2014.

Bohannan, Laura [Eleanor Smith Bowen]. *Return to Laughter* [1954]. New York: Natural History Museum, 1964.

Brecht, Bertolt. *Bertolt Brecht: Poems, 1913–1956*. Edited by John Willett and Ralph Manheim with Erich Fried. London: Methuen, 1976; revised edition, New York: Routledge, 1987.

Caillois, Roger. *Man and the Sacred* [1950]. Urbana: University of Illinois Press, 2001.

———. "Mimicry and Legendary Psychasthenia" [1935]. Translated by John Shepley. *October*, no. 31 (1984): 16–32.

Calderón de la Barca, Pedro. *Life Is a Dream* [1629–1635]. Translated by Edward Fitzgerald. http://www.gutenberg.org/ebooks/6363.

Cannon, Walter B. *The Wisdom of the Body*. New York: Norton, 1932.

Caygill, Howard. *On Resistance: A Philosophy of Defiance*. London: Bloomsbury, 2013.

Cervantes, Miguel de. *Don Quixote de la Mancha*. Translated by Peter Motteux. New York: Random House, 1941.

Chapman, Anne. *Hain: Initiation Ceremony of the Selknam of Tierra Del Fuego* [2002]. Buenos Aires: Zagier & Urruty, 2008.

Clifford, James. *Person and Myth: Maurice Leenhardt in the Melanesian World*. Berkeley: University of California Press, 1982.

Comey, James. "How Trump Co-opts Leaders Like Bill Barr." *New York Times*, May 2, 2019.

Davis, Mike. *Dead Cities: A Natural History*. New York: New Press, 2002.

Deleuze, Gilles, and Félix Guattari. *A Thousand Plateaus: Capitalism and Schizophrenia* [1980]. Translated by Brian Massumi. Minneapolis: University of Minnesota Press, 1987.

Dickinson, Emily. "The Last Night That She Lived." In *The Selected Poems of Emily Dickinson*, 207. New York: Modern Library, 1996.

Didi-Huberman, Georges. *L'image survivante*. Paris: Éditions de Minuit, 2002.

———. *Survivance des lucioles*. Paris: Éditions de Minuit, 2009.

———. *The Surviving Image: Phantoms of Time and Time of Phantoms: Aby Warburg's History of Art*. Translated by Harvey Mendelsohn. University Park: Pennsylvania State University Press, 2016.

Dorson, Richard M. "The Eclipse of Solar Mythology." *Journal of American Folklore* 68, no. 270 (1955): 393–416.

Dostoevsky, Fyodor. *Crime and Punishment*. Foreword by Richard Pevear. New York: Vintage, 1991.

Emerson, Ralph Waldo. "Nature." In *Essays and Lectures*. New York: Library of America, 1983.

Fermor, Patrick Leigh. *Mani: Travels in the Southern Peloponnese* [1968]. New York: New York Review Books, 2006.

Flaubert, Gustave. *The Temptation of Saint Anthony*. Translated by Kitty Mrosovsky. 1874; Harmondsworth: Penguin, 1983.

Foucault, Michel. *Language, Counter-Memory, Practice: Selected Essays and Interviews* [1963]. Edited by Donald F. Bouchard. Translated by Donald F. Bouchard and Sherry Simon. Ithaca, NY: Cornell University Press, 1977.

Frazer, James George. *The Golden Bough: A Study in Magic and Religion*. 3rd ed., revised and enlarged. London: Macmillan, 1920.

Griffith, Erin. "What's Their Sign? It's the Dollar Sign." *New York Times*, International Edition, April 19, 2019.

Gysin, Brion, and Terry Wilson. *Here to Go: Planet R-101*. San Francisco: Re/Search Publications, 1982.

Hansen, Miriam Bratu. *Cinema and Experience: Siegfried Kracauer, Walter Benjamin, and Theodor W. Adorno*. Berkeley: University of California Press, 2011.

Harambour, Alberto. *Un viaje a las colonias: Memorias y diario de un overjero escoses en Malvinas, Patagonia y Tierra del Fuego (1878-1898)*. Santiago: Dirección de Bibliotecas, Archivos y Museos, 2016.

Haraway, Donna. *The Companion Species Manifesto*. Chicago: Prickly Paradigm, 2003.

Hollier, Denis, ed. *The College of Sociology, 1937-1939*. Minneapolis: University of Minnesota Press, 1988.

Horkheimer, Max, and Theodor W. Adorno. *Dialectic of Enlightenment*. Edited by Gunzelin Schmid Noerr. Translated by Edmund Jephcott. Stanford, CA: Stanford University Press, 2002.

Jameson, Fredric. *Late Marxism: Adorno, or the Persistence of the Dialectic* [1990]. New York: Verso, 2007.

Junod, Henri. *The Life of a South African Tribe* [1912]. 2 vols. Hyde Park: University Books, 1962.

Kafka, Franz. *Kafka: The Complete Stories*. Edited by Nahum N. Glatzer. New York: Schocken, 1971.

Kahn, Douglas. *John Heartfield: Art and Mass Media*. New York: Tanam Press, 1985.

Khayyat, Munia. "A Landscape of War: On the Nature of Violence in South Lebanon." PhD thesis. Department of Anthropology, Columbia University, 2013.

Lawrence, D. H. *Apocalypse and the Writings on Revelation*. Edited by Mara Klanins. Cambridge: Cambridge University Press, 2002.

Lebel, Robert, and Isabelle Waldberg, eds. *Encyclopaedia Acephalica*. London: Atlas Press, 1995.

Le Guin, Ursula K. "Great Nature's Second Course." In *Words Are My Matter: Writings about Life and Books, 2000-2016*. Easthampton: Small Beer Press, 2016.

Levi-Strauss, David. *Between Dog and Wolf: Essays on Art and Politics in the Twilight of the Millennium*. Brooklyn: Autonomedia, 1998.

Lucas, George. *Star Wars*. New York: Ballantine, 1976.

Lundberg, Johanna. *Finnish Landscape*. Helsinki: Garret, 2016.

Mahler, Jonathan, and Jim Rutenberg. "How Rupert Murdoch's Empire of Influence Remade the World." *New York Times*, April 3, 2019.

Malinowski, Bronislaw. *A Diary in the Strict Sense of the Term*. 2nd ed. [1967]. London: Althone, 1989.

———. *Coral Gardens and Their Magic*, vol. 1 [1935]. Bloomington: Indiana University Press, 1965.

Marx, Karl, and Friedrich Engels. *The German Ideology. Part One, with Selections from Part Two and Three and Supplementary Texts*. Edited by C. J. Arthur. New York: International Publishers, 1970.

Mauss, Marcel. *The Gift*. Translated by Ian Cunnison. London: Cohen & West, 1966.

Melville, Herman. *Moby-Dick; or, The Whale*. Edited by Harrison Hayford, Hershel

Parker, and G. Thomas Tanselle. Evanston, IL: Northwestern University Press, 1994.

Michelson, Annette. "Heterology and the Critique of Instrumental Reason." *October*, no. 36 (1986): 111-27.

Moe, Aaron M. *Zoopoetics: Animals and the Making of Poetry*. Lanham, MD: Lexington Press, 2014.

Newell, Sasha. *The Modernity Bluff: Crime, Consumption, and Citizenship in Côte d'Ivoire*. Chicago: University of Chicago Press, 2012.

Nietzsche, Friedrich. "Attempt at a Self-Criticism." In *The Birth of Tragedy and The Case of Wagner*. Translated by Walter Kaufmann. New York: Random House, 1967.

———. *The Gay Science: With a Prelude in Rhymes and an Appendix of Songs*. Edited by Bernard Williams. Translated by Josefine Nauckhoff. Cambridge: Cambridge University Press, 2001.

———. "On the Use and Abuse of History for Life." In *Untimely Meditations*, edited by Daniel Breazeale. Translated by R. J. Hollingdale. Cambridge: Cambridge University Press, 1997.

———. *Thus Spoke Zarathustra*. Translated by R. J. Hollingdale. London: Penguin, 1961.

———. *Twilight of the Idols and The Anti-Christ; or, How to Philosophize with a Hammer*. Edited by Michael Tanner. Translated by R. J. Hollingdale. New York: Penguin, 1990.

Nordenskiöld, Erland, and Ruben Pérez Kantule. *An Historical and Ethnographic Study of the Cuna Indians*. Edited by Henry Wassen. Göteborg: Etnografiskamuseet, 1938.

Ollman, Bertell. *Alienation: Marx's Concept of Man in Capitalist Society*. Cambridge: Cambridge University Press, 1971.

Pasolini, Pier Paolo. "Il vuoto del potere in Italia." *Corriere della Sera*, February 1, 1975.

Proust, Marcel. *In Search of Lost Time*. Vol. 1, *Swann's Way*. Translated by Lydia Davis. New York: Viking, 2003.

———. *In Search of Lost Time*. Vol. 2, *Within a Budding Grove*. Translated by C. K. Scott Moncrieff and Terence Kilmartin. Revised by D. J. Enright. New York: Modern Library, 1993.

———. *In Search of Lost Time*. Vol. 3, *The Guermantes Way*. Translated by C. K. Scott Moncrieff and Terence Kilmartin. Revised by D. J. Enright. New York: Modern Library, 1993.

———. *In Search of Lost Time*. Vol. 4, *Sodom and Gomorrah*. Translated by C. K. Scott Moncrieff and Terence Kilmartin. Revised by D. J. Enright. New York: Modern Library, 1993.

———. *In Search of Lost Time*. Vol. 5, *The Captive*. Translated by C. K. Scott Moncrieff and Terence Kilmartin. Revised by D. J. Enright. New York: Modern Library, 1993.

———. *In Search of Lost Time*. Vol. 6, *Time Regained*. Translated by Andreas Mayor and Terence Kilmartin. Revised by D. J. Enright. New York: Modern Library, 1993.

Pynchon, Thomas. *Gravity's Rainbow* [1973]. New York: Penguin, 1995.

Reichel-Dolmatoff, Gerardo, and Alicia Reichel-Dolmatoff. *The People of Aritama: The Cultural Personality of a Colombian Mestizo Village*. London: Routledge, 1961.

Sahlins, Marshall. "The Hau in the Gift." In *Stone Age Economics*. Chicago: Aldine-Atherton, 1972.

Santner, Eric. *On Creaturely Life: Rilke, Benjamin, Sebald*. Chicago: University of Chicago Press, 2006.

Shaviro, Steven. *The Cinematic Body*. Minneapolis: University of Minnesota Press, 1993.

Standage, Tom. *The Turk: The Life and Times of the Famous Eighteenth-Century Chess Playing Machine*. New York: Walker, 2002.

Taussig, Michael. *Defacement: Public Secrecy and the Labor of the Negative*. Stanford, CA: Stanford University Press, 1999.

———. "The Go Slow Party." In *The Corn Wolf*. Chicago: University of Chicago Press, 2015.

———. *Law in a Lawless Land*. Chicago: University of Chicago Press, 2003.

———. *Mimesis and Alterity*. London: Routledge, 1993.

———. *My Cocaine Museum*. Chicago: University of Chicago Press, 2004.

———. *Palma Africana*. Chicago: University of Chicago Press, 2018.

———. *Palma de aceite colombiana*. Bogotá: Villegas Editores, 2013.

———. *Shamanism, Colonialism, and the Wild Man*. Chicago: University of Chicago Press, 1987.

———. "Viscerality, Faith, and Skepticism: Another Theory of Magic" [1998]. In *Walter Benjamin's Grave*. Chicago: University of Chicago Press, 2006. Also in *HAU: Journal of Ethnographic Theory* 6, no. 3 (2016), https://www.haujournal.org/index.php/hau/article/view/hau6.3.033.

———. *What Color Is the Sacred?* Chicago: University of Chicago Press, 2009.

Tayler, Donald. *The Coming of the Sun, a Prologue to Ika Sacred Narrative*. Pitt-Rivers Museum Monograph no. 7. Oxford: University of Oxford, 1997.

Turner, Victor. *In the Forest of Symbols: Aspects of Ndembu Ritual*. Ithaca, NY: Cornell University Press, 1967.

Valero, Vicente. *Experiencia y pobreza: Benjamin en Ibiza, 1932–1933*. Barcelona: Ediciones Peninsula, 2001.

Vico, Giambattista. *The New Science of Giambattista Vico* [1725–1744]. Translated by Thomas G. Bergin and Max H. Fisch. Ithaca, NY: Cornell University Press, 1970.

Wallace, David Foster. "How Tracy Austin Broke My Heart." In *Consider the Lobster and Other Essays*. New York: Little, Brown and Company, 2005.

Weigel, Sigrid. *Body and Image-Space: Re-Reading Walter Benjamin*. London: Routledge, 1996.

Wilbert, Johannes. "The Origin of the Women's Kloketen." In *Folk Literature of the Selknam Indians; Martin Gusinde's Collection of Selknam Narratives*, pp. 147–61. Los Angeles: UCLA Latin America Center Publications, 1975.

Young, Michael. *Malinowski: Odyssey of an Anthropologist, 1884–1920*. New Haven, CT: Yale University Press, 2004.

FILMS

Les maîtres fous, dir. Jean Rouch (1955).

The Servant, dir. Joseph Losey (1963).

Trobriand Cricket: An Ingenious Response to Colonialism, dir. Gary Kildea and Jerry W. Leach (1976).

INDEX

Made in the USA
Middletown, DE
29 October 2023

41402605R00137